Scottish Nationalism and Cultural Identity in the Twentieth Century

Scottish Nationalism and Cultural Identity in the Twentieth Century

An Annotated Bibliography of Secondary Sources

Compiled by
GORDON BRYAN

Bibliographies and Indexes in Law and Political Science, Number 1

Greenwood Press
Westport, Connecticut • London, England

Library of Congress Cataloging in Publication Data

Bryan, Gordon.
   Scottish nationalism and cultural identity in the
twentieth century.

   (Bibliographies and indexes in law and political
science, ISSN 0742-6909 ; no. 1)
   Includes index.
   1. Nationalism—Scotland—Bibliography.   2. Scotland—
Politics and government—20th century—Bibliography.
I. Title. II. Series.
Z2067.N35B79 1984   [DA821]   016.306'09411   84-4667
ISBN 0-313-23998-3 (lib. bdg.)

Library of Congress Catalog Card Number: 84-4667
ISBN: 0-313-23998-3
ISSN: 0742-6909

First published in 1984

Greenwood Press
A division of Congressional Information Service, Inc.
88 Post Road West, Westport, Connecticut 06881

Printed in the United States of America

10 9 8 7 6 5 4 3 2 1

To Valerie

CONTENTS

INTRODUCTION

Scotland's ancient sovereignty ended in 1707 with
Parliamentary Union with England. Since then, there has
never been a dearth of writing about Scotland's sense of
political and cultural "separateness" within the United
Kingdom. Today there is a vast literature of Scottish
alienation.

A bibliography can provide a useful "state of the art"
by reducing an unwieldy subject to manageable proportions.
But there are other good reasons for a bibliography on
Scottish Nationalism and culture.

Existing bibliographies on this theme generally work
from within a framework of nationalism or British politics.
They are usually restricted by time and space and can
only include a limited selection. P.D. Hancock's <u>A
Bibliography of Works Relating to Scotland 1916-1950</u> (1959)
and Eric G. Grant's <u>Scotland</u> (ABC-Clio, 1982) are two
such examples, with Grant's work focusing on works
published since 1960.

Many also concentrate exclusively on politics and ignore
the cultural dimension completely. Major Scottish writers
are never mentioned and crucial questions of language and
art vis a vis political nationalism are never considered.

The strongest argument for a "state of the art" list is
the exclusion of Scottish Studies from most traditional
English departments and courses in schools and universities
in Great Britain and North America. (Hugh MacDiarmid saw
this exclusion as deliberate racism, prompting him to list
one of his hobbies in a <u>Who's Who</u> as Anglophobia!)
Whatever the reasons for this exclusion, students and
teachers who do wish more information should have openings
to further study. In the United States, the excellent
teaching in Scottish Studies in places such as Old Dominion
University, the University of South Carolina, and the
University of Massachusetts proves the desire to end that
exclusion.

Moreover, the popular romantic symbols of Scotland--kilts, clans, bagpipes, Loch Ness Monsters, and Bonnie Prince Charlie--have created a veritable "Tartan Curtain" beyond which few are willing to see some of the worst slums in Europe, alarmingly high levels of crime and alcoholism, one of the poorest health records in Northern Europe, and rural ghettoes comparable to the worst pockets of Appalachia; all amid scenery unrivalled for beauty. A very substantial literature written by Scots and others who wish to solve these problems is the more worthy of a hearing.

Kenneth C. Fraser's <u>Bibliography of the Scottish National Movement 1844-1973</u> is a comprehensive work on Scottish Nationalism to that date, with its excellent list of historic pamphlets and journals. He employs a thematic approach that extends to poetry and fiction. His unannotated bibliography has a strong nineteenth century emphasis and is of special benefit to those having access to the works he lists, most of which would be difficult to find outside the major libraries of Edinburgh and Glasgow.

My concentration on the twentieth century stresses the present dynamism of Scottish politics and culture and restores a balance to writing on Scotland that ends with Hume and Burns or Scott and Stevenson, while ignoring recent important developments like the Scottish Renaissance of the 1920s or the ideas of John MacLean.

This bibliography thus fills a gap by being both lengthy and annotated as well as current. The 894 annotated items are articles, pamphlets, books, and book chapters from works appearing in Britain and the United States between 1900 and 1983. Most of these are secondary sources; many were taken from original sources that have not been described or annotated elsewhere.

It is not easy to reduce a century of writing to a neat and tidy list of basic sources. Compromise was necessary between variety and thoroughness, the left and the right, pro and con, extremism and moderation, and most of all, between quality and quantity. I concentrated on journals that had long runs or were influential in their day, or that produced leading articles by cultural figures like Lewis Spence, Hugh MacDiarmid, Neil Gunn, Edwin Muir, and others. However, attention was also paid to the businessman, the local politician, and the man in the street. Arguments against Scottish Nationalism were surprisingly few, but were included to give balance.

The organization of the book was suggested by the pattern of the annotations. General articles seemed more useful when listed chronologically--first by monographs, then by serials. The dates represent key developments in Scottish politics or culture or in world affairs.

Other items demanded a thematic treatment and seemed less affected by time changes. For example, the arguments for the revival of Gaelic in 1910 are not very different from the same arguments in 1935 or 1983.

The chapter on language revival provides a very useful background, highlighting the cultural dimension of Scottish Nationalism that is frequently ignored or misunderstood.

The chapter on "Models" is unique and probably is a first listing of sources in this way. Because culture and language are more closely welded together in other countries than in Scotland, many articles on language revival appear in this chapter as well.

Hugh MacDiarmid certainly warranted an entire chapter, for his output was extraordinary. It may never be fully described with certainty, owing to his penchant for pseudonyms. I went to many early journals for these articles. My list is only representative but some of the pieces on fascism or social credit have never been described or annotated and are an original feature of the list.

Although I have tried to avoid much emphasis on any one political party, the Scottish National Party (SNP) probably receives more attention because of its longevity. I have tried to portray a "mosaic" of many partyless individuals, groups, clubs, and so forth, that have been involved in the issue of Scottish independence.

The citations give data required for purchase, for finding in libraries, or for acquiring through interlibrary loan. Where volume numbers may have changed or are not consistent, as in the Scots Independent, I have omitted them. I have listed data for the book at hand but not for reprints and revisions.

Spelling has posed problems. Generally, I have used American spelling, but have retained British spellings when they are part of quotes or titles, or for convenience in words like "Labour Party" or "programme. I have also adopted a few spellings to avoid confusion, as when I capitalize Scottish Nationalism to distinguish it from nationalism in general.

As a Canadian-born, half-Scot, American citizen living in England, I have aimed at broad appeal and interest. The subjects touched upon--British history, language, socialism and nationalism, minority rights, cultural dominance--have as much relevance to American and Canadian relations and politics as they do to European society. I have tried to keep students and scholars and librarians and libraries in mind when compiling this list.

My main purpose has been to parade through the decades as wide a range of topics, individuals, and sources as possible, and to provide more openings to a fascinating and timely subject.

Unfortunately, selection presupposes judgment and judgment involves error. Omissions are inevitable. Some sources were incomplete or not available when I needed them. Others made annotation impossible. However, all errors and misunderstandings are entirely my own.

Bibliographers are by nature dependent, and I am especially thankful for the editorial advice and patience of Mary R. Sive, Acquisitions Editor at Greenwood Press.

Also, I found it satisfying to observe the high level of service so typical (but so often unappreciated) of librarians everywhere I worked. I thank the staff of the Chester, England, Public Library for valuable interlibrary loan assistance. I owe special thanks to the staffs of the Mitchell Library in Glasgow, the Edinburgh Public Library, and the National Library of Scotland.

So, having borrowed freely of the time and work of others, I offer this work up in turn for someone else's benefit, criticism, or improvement and hope that it might aid future study as part of the ever-turning bibliographic wheel.

Scottish Nationalism and Cultural Identity in the Twentieth Century

1.

BIBLIOGRAPHY OF BIBLIOGRAPHIES

Many bibliographies treat Scottish Nationalism only as part of a broader subject, e.g. Scottish Politics or World Nationalism. Many of the ones I list fall into this category. Bibliographies on pertinent issues or individuals are also listed in order to add scope and variety and to provide as many opportunities and approaches to further study as possible.

SCOTTISH NATIONALISM SPECIFICALLY

1. Fraser, Kenneth C. A Bibliography of the Scottish National Movement 1844-1973. Dollar, Scotland: Douglas S. Mack, 1976. 40pp.

> 539 items listed under several headings: history, legal aspects, fiction, and many more. Not annotated. Lists periodicals with volume dates and numbers and periodicals and pamphlets produced by various nationalist bodies. Strong historical and 19th century emphasis. Also lists works that contain chapters on Scottish Nationalism. Useful thematic approach.

2. Hanham, Harry J. "Bibliography." In Scottish Nationalism. London: Faber, 1969, 232-240.

> Approximately 100 sources listed, including useful information on early nationalist periodicals and on the R.E. Muirhead Collection in the National Library of Scotland.

3. Webb, Keith. "Bibliography." In The Growth of Nationalism
in Scotland. Glasgow: Molendinar Press, 1977, 137-140.

   Select bibliography, 75 items. Books, periodicals, and
   secondary sources for the general reader. Not annotated.
   Mostly material from the 1960's and 1970's. Includes
   dissertations, unpublished papers, and conference
   proceedings. Lists most standard works.

SCOTTISH POLITICS IN GENERAL, INCLUDING NATIONALISM

4. Allen, C. H. "Bibliography." In Our Changing Scotland:
a Yearbook of Scottish Government 1976-77, edited by M.G.
Clarke and H.M. Drucker, 110-131. Edinburgh: Edinburgh
University Student Bureau, 1976.

   Fairly complete bibliography of 707 items appearing
   between May 1, 1975, and April 30, 1976. Books,
   pamphlets, newspaper articles and features, with
   subject index and day-to-day coverage. Many of these
   deal with Scottish Nationalism.

5. Allen, C.H. "Bibliography." In The Scottish Government
Yearbook 1979, edited by N. Drucker and H.M. Drucker, 158-
197. Edinburgh: EUSB, 1979.

   Fairly complete list of 1045 items on Scottish politics
   appearing between June 6, 1977, and May 31, 1978.
   Divided into "Books, Pamphlets, and Longer Articles" and
   "Short Items".

6. Allen, C.H. "Bibliography." In The Scottish Government
Yearbook 1980, edited by H.M. Drucker and N.L. Drucker,
280-319. Edinburgh: Paul Harris, 1979.

   "Recent Publications in Scottish Government and
   Politics." 952 articles, books, and pamphlets appearing
   up to May 31, 1978. Articles on Scottish Nationalism
   and devolution are included.

7. Allen, C.H. "Bibliography." In The Scottish Government
Yearbook 1981, edited by H.M. Drucker and N.L. Drucker,
306-328. Edinburgh: Paul Harris, 1981.

   A select but thorough listing of 399 items on Scottish
   politics appearing between June 1, 1979, and May 31,
   1980. Newspaper articles, pamphlets, and books, with
   good coverage of Scottish Nationalism.

8. Allen, C.H. "Bibliography." In The Scottish Government Yearbook 1982, edited by H.M. Drucker and N.L. Drucker, 313-340. Edinburgh: Paul Harris, 1981.

    A select list of 487 items on Scottish politics appearing between June 1, 1980, and May 31, 1981. Newspaper articles, pamphlets and books, many having a bearing on Scottish Nationalism.

9. Allen, C.H. "Bibliography." In The Scottish Government Yearbook 1983, edited by David McCrone, 277-299. Edinburgh: EUSG, 1982.

    A comprehensive bibliography of articles, pamphlets and books appearing between June 1, 1981, and May 31, 1982. 384 items. Allen's bibliography is especially good for tracking down major newspaper articles. Nationalism and devolution appear often.

10. Kellas, James G. "Bibliography." In Modern Scotland: The Nation Since 1870. London: Pall Mall, 1968, 252-258.

    A short select bibliography of articles and government publications on Scotland, only a few of which deal with Scottish Nationalism.

11. Mercer, John. "Bibliography." In Scotland: the Devolution of Power. London: John Calder, 1978.

    A short select bibliography of about 70 entries. Periodical articles on devolution and regional reform are listed.

12. National Library of Scotland. Bibliography of Scotland 1981. Edinburgh: National Library of Scotland, 1982. 388pp.

    The fifth annual volume. Listing of works published after 1975, processed during 1981 by the National Library. Material all relates to Scotland. Topographical and subject arrangement. For finding references to Scottish Nationalism, see:
"Scotland - Politics and Government - 20th Century"
"Nationalism - Scotland"
"Decentralization in Government - Scotland"
Not annotated. Includes list of jounals and publishers for Scottish works. These annual volumes are available from the National Library.

13. Pollock, Lawrence, and McAllister, Ian. A Bibliography of U.K. Politics: Scotland, Wales and Northern Ireland. Glasgow: University of Strathclyde Centre for the Study of Public Policy, 1980. 126pp.

    A fairly comprehensive select bibliography dealing with United Kingdom politics in the 1970's.

NATIONALISM IN GENERAL, INCLUDING SCOTTISH NATIONALISM

14.   Davis, Horace B. "Bibliography." In Nationalism and
Socialism: Marxist and Labor Theories of Nationalism to 1917.
NY: Monthly Review Press, 1967, 237-243.

> A select bibliography dealing with Marxist views of the
> nation and of self-determination. Concentrates on Marx,
> Engels, and Lenin. Sources in French and German also
> included. Many items are pertinent to Scottish left-
> wing nationalism.

15.   Seton-Watson, Hugh. "Bibliography." In Nations and
States: an inquiry into the origins of nations and the
politics of nationalism. London: Methuen, 1977, 507-544.

> Select bibliography on nationalism, with books and
> other sources arranged by nation or region. Also, works
> dealing with the concept of nationhood are listed.
> There is a section on Scottish Nationalism.

16.   Smith, Anthony D.S. "Bibliography." In Nationalism in
the Twentieth Century. Oxford: Martin Robertson, 1979, 229-
243.

> A select bibliography of books and journal articles,
> international in scope, covering nationalism in all
> aspects. Lengthy and thorough, valuable to all students
> of nationalism. Some essential works on Scottish
> Nationalism are covered.

17.   Snyder, Louis L. "Bibliography." In Global Mini-
Nationalisms: Autonomy or Independence. Westport, Conn:
Greenwood Press, 1982, 303-312.

> Books and periodicals. Nationalism in general. 300
> entries from all time periods, and in various
> languages, including works on Scottish Nationalism.

18.   Thomson, Ian. Devolution: A Guide to Sources of
Information. Pontypridd: Polytechnic of Wales Library, 1979,
25pp.

> A select, annotated bibliography on the Polytechnic's
> holdings on devolution, with strong emphasis on Wales,
> but including Scotland. Books, pamphlets, indexes,
> abstracts and Government publications. Updated often.
> Excellent general sources and useful core list. Has
> strong library emphasis, thus especially helpful for
> library collection building.

INDIVIDUALS AND THEMES RELEVANT TO SCOTTISH NATIONALISM

19. Aitken, W.R. "A Hugh MacDiarmid Bibliography." In
Hugh MacDiarmid: a Critical Survey, edited by Duncan Glen,
228-241. Edinburgh: Scottish Academic Press, 1972.

   A comprehensive listing of Hugh MacDiarmid's works,
   over 90 books written by or about him. Aitken's is the
   definitive bibliography on MacDiarmid.

20. Ellis, P. Beresford. "Bibliography." In James Connolly:
Selected Writings. NY: Monthly Review Press, 1974, 309-311.

   Select bibliography of Connolly's writings, and
   works dealing with Connolly's life, ideas, and
   influence on nationalism and socialism. His ideas on
   language, small nations, nationalism and internationalism,
   and British imperialism are pertinent to Scottish
   Nationalism. Connolly was Scottish-born and active in
   socialist movements there.

21. Glen, Duncan. "Bibliography." In Hugh MacDiarmid and
the Scottish Renaissance. Edinburgh: Chambers, 1964, 245-
294.

   A bibliography of MacDiarmid's books, pamphlets,
   translations, editorials, uncollected prose, and
   criticism of his work by other poets. This is an
   excellent source for some of MacDiarmid's lesser-
   known political prose and polemic.

22. MacKinnon, Kenneth. "Bibliography." In The Lion's
Tongue. Inverness: Club Leabhar, 1974, 120-123.

   Select bibliography of 100 books and articles on the
   Gaelic language and culture of Scotland with special
   attention paid to its revival and future.

23. Price, Glanville. The Present Position of Minority
Languages in Western Europe: A Selective Bibliography.
Cardiff: University of Wales, 1969. 81pp.

   Sources on Scots and on Scottish Gaelic, as well as
   other languages such as Basque, Catalan, and Breton.

24. Stephens, Meic. "Selected Bibliography." In Linguistic
Minorities in Western Europe. Llandysul: Gomer, 1976, 739-
767.

   Arranged by nation and by language. Strong emphasis on
   politics and cultural nationalism. Good general sources
   on languages in Scotland and on Scottish Nationalism.

2.

1900–1939: BIRTH, MERGER, SCHISM

That the two kingdoms of Scotland and England shall, upon
the 1st of May next ensuing the date hereof and for ever
after, be united into one Kingdom by the name of Great
Britain.

Treaty of Union
16 January, 1707

The century began with heated debate on Irish and Scottish
Home Rule, with several substantial Home Rule bills being
introduced in Parliament. World War I slowed the impetus for
Home Rule, but many Scots returning from a war fought in
part for the rights of small nations found themselves
disillusioned with Scotland's own status. The 1920's saw a
remarkable political and cultural rebirth in Scotland, lead
by intellectuals like Hugh MacDiarmid, Lewis Spence, Compton
MacKenzie, Edwin Muir, and others. This cultural foment
resulted in the founding of the Scottish National Party in
1934. This alliance of nationalists was never an easy one,
and defections and expulsions were many. By 1939, the number
of Scottish National Party members had dropped to 2,000 from
10,000 in 1934. World War II split Scottish socialists and
nationalists into many camps, aggravating differences between
left and right, militant and moderate, separatist and
devolutionist, literature and politics. These divisions
have remained to this day.

BOOKS AND PAMPHLETS

25. Bell, William. Rip Van Scotland. London: Cecil Palmer,
1930. 147pp.

> A strangely prophetic work, calling for Scotland to
> strike for freedom before war breaks out, arguing that
> strict wartime measures will crush any attempts at
> Scottish independence.

26. Black, Charles Stewart. The Case for Scotland. Glasgow: Glasgow University Nationalist Association, 1931. 24pp.

Arguments for Scottish self-government with a Federal Britain. Rationale for the National Party of Scotland as the best party to secure federalism for Scotland.

27. Black, Charles Stewart. Scottish Nationalism: Its Inspiration and Its Aims. Glasgow: National Party of Scotland, 1934. 32pp.

The program of the National Party of Scotland and its goal "to secure the complete independence of Scotland, within the British Commonwealth."

28. Bowie, James A. The Future of Scotland. London: Chambers, 1939. 272pp. bibl.

Bowie documents Scotland's major economic problems - inadequate housing, poor health care, declining industry - and proposes solutions based on greater autonomy for Scotland. Statistics and forecasts now outdated, but the work has historical interest. Bibliography outdated.

29. Brown, W. Oliver. Scotland and Westminster. Glasgow: Labour Council for Scottish Self-Government, 1939. 20pp.

A collection of quotes and newspaper clippings showing abuse of power at Westminster, concluding that "a Scottish government is necessary for the application of socialism."

30. Erskine, Ruaridh. Changing Scotland. Montrose: Review Press, 1931. 73pp.

Erskine favors a Celtic culture and state with the Gaelic language at the fore. Scottish independence must ensure a lasting revival of ancient Celtic institutions, he argues, here and in many other writings. A strong case is made for cultural nationalism.

31. Gibb, Andrew D. Scotland in Eclipse. London: Toulmin, 1930. 200pp.

An account of the major problems in the Scotland of Gibb's time: depopulation, emigration, poverty, the weakening of Scots law, and others. Although much is outdated, Gibb provides insight into nationalist thought between the Wars.

32. McCallum, R. Home Rule for Scotland. Blenheim: W. and J. Barr, 1925. 30pp.

A justification for Home Rule. Explanations intended for Scots living in Australia and New Zealand.

33. MacEwen, Alexander M. The Thistle and the Rose:
Scotland's Problem Today. Edinburgh: Oliver and Boyd, 1932.
244 pp.

The author thinks that a Scottish Parliament can alone
solve Scotland's critical problems. MacEwen advocates
bilingualism and devotes several pages to the "Highland
Problem." The work serves as a key to the general
Scottish political debate of the 1930's.

34. MacEwen, Alexander M. Towards Freedom: a Candid Survey
of Fascism, Communism, and Modern Democracy. London: William
Hodge and Company, 1938. 244pp.

MacEwen urges Scottish nationalists to avoid the many
evils of nationalism. He stresses "genuine nationalism"-
one based on spiritual and political liberty. He sees
Norway and Denmark as models of small nations with rich
cultures. Devolution is MacEwen's political ideal for
Scotland.

35. Maclehose, Alexander. The Scotland of Our Sons. Glasgow:
Maclehose, 1937. 302pp.

How a Scottish Parliament would improve fishing and
forestries, reverse rural decay and urban poverty, and
revitalize the Highlands. Statistics have historical
interest.

36. Power, William. My Scotland. Edinburgh: Porpoise Press,
1934. 303pp.

General articles first appearing in the Daily Record and
Glasgow Evening News on all features of Scottish politics
and culture by a celebrated Scottish journalist and
nationalist.

37. Power, William. Should Auld Acquaintance. London: Harrap,
1937. 256pp.

Power gives excellent portraits of literary and political
figures, including C. M. Grieve and Cunninghame-Graham.
Biography covers Power's involvement with Glasgow's
political life in the 1920's.

38. Scottish National Party. Post War Scotland: a survey of
Scotland's political, economic and cultural position.
Glasgow; SNP, 1934. 14pp.

In form of a letter to a visitor to Scotland.

39. Scottish National Party. Self Government for Scotland.
Glasgow: SNP, 1935. 6pp.

> Also in Gaelic. Four major points: Scotland will have a
> Parliament, will remain part of the Commonwealth, will
> co-operate with British Customs and Defence, and will
> insist upon the independence of the Scottish National
> Party from all other parties.

40. Spence, Lewis. Freedom for Scotland: the Case for
Scottish Self-Government. Edinburgh: The Scottish National
Movement, 1926. 42pp.

> Spence, a poet and anthropologist, argues for Home Rule
> on historical, biological, and psychological grounds,
> as well as seeing it as the only cure for emigration,
> slums, and Scotland's chronic unemployment.

41. Spence, Lewis. The National Party of Scotland. Glasgow:
National Party of Scotland, 1928. 18 pp.

> A statement of the origins and aims of the National
> Party of Scotland, founded in 1928 by Spence and other
> leading Scottish intellectuals. This party merged with
> the Scottish Party in 1934 to form the Scottish National
> Party.

42. Thomson, George. The Kingdom of Scotland Restored.
London: Toulmin, 1935. 24pp.

> Thomson urges a "new nationalism"-modern, creative, and
> self-critical, yet wedded to practical politics.

43. Walkinshaw, Colin. The Scots Tragedy. London: Routledge,
1935. 209pp.

> Walkinshaw (pseudonym for James M. Reid) presents a
> general history of Scotland from a nationalist viewpoint.

44. Wood, Wendy. I Like Life. Edinburgh: Moray Press, 1938.
309pp.

> Wood, a popular nationalist of long standing, brings
> her biography up to the 1930's. See especially chapter
> titles "Nationalism" and "Ireland."

45. Young Scots Society. National Manifesto on Scottish
Home Rule. Glasgow: Young Scots Society, 1912.

> The Society's position in favor of Home Rule for Ireland
> and Scotland.

46. Young Scots Society. Sixty Points for Scottish Home
Rule. Glasgow: Maclaren, 1912. 72pp.

This pamphlet considers emigration, rural decay, housing,
education, and the relevance of Irish Home Rule to
Scottish Home Rule. A comprehensive argument for Home
Rule in general.

47. Young Scots Society. Young Scots Handbook. Glasgow:
The Young Scots Society, 1912. 112pp.

A sketch of the Young Scots Society's history and of
Home Rule in Scotland, Wales, and Ireland.

ARTICLES

48. Cammell, Charles R. "Scottish Independence from Three
Points of View." Scots Independent (September 1931): 164.

The writer believes that Scottish Nationalism will not
only benefit Scotland but will contribute to the world
harmony that might result in the co-operation of small
nations versus the imperialism of the great nations.
Cammell argues that smaller nations have a firmer moral
base than large states.

49. Clark, Angus. "Nationalists Must Unite." New Scotland 1
(February 1936): 1.

A call for the unity of the various parties supporting
Scottish independence.

50. Cunninghame-Graham, R.B. "McSneeshin." Scots Independent
(January 1931): 36.

Cunninghame-Graham sketches a true enemy of Scottish
culture and change: "McSneeshin" the smug, unimaginative,
complacent Scot who supports the status quo in all things.

51. Donaldson, Arthur. "Land Settlement: a Challenge to
Scottish Manhood." Scots Independent (December 1931): 21.

Twelve owners owned 25% of Scotland and 1700 persons
owned 90% of the land in 1931. Donaldson argues for
immediate and radical agrarian reform, citing
Czechoslovakia and Mexico as successful examples.

52. Donaldson, Arthur. "The Material and Spiritual Poverty
of the Scottish Nation." Scots Independent (November 1930):
10.

Donaldson cites political opression, religion, and
capitalism as the reasons for Scotland's plight.

53. Donaldson, Arthur. "The Rise of Scottish Nationalism."
Scots Independent (February 1933): 60.

   Donaldson finds Scottish Nationalism in the 1930's
   a very complex subject. By contrast, he believes the
   old Home Rule movements were much simpler in aims and
   methods.

54. Donaldson, Arthur. "The Scot Abroad." Scots Independent
(January 1930): 27.

   Resident in Detroit in the 1930's, Donaldson found
   overseas Scots vastly uninformed about Scotland's
   political and social struggles.

55. Donaldson, Arthur. "The Scottish Neutrality League."
Scots Independent (December 1938): 31

   The League is explained: its goal to preserve Scots
   neutrality and to aid conscientious objectors in any
   future wars.

56. Donaldson, Arthur. "Towards a National Policy." Scots
Independent (June 1931): 120.

   Donaldson supports preparation at the local and city
   government levels so that the switch to national
   independence will be done smoothly, with trained
   staff.

57. Donaldson, Sir James. "Home Rule and Scottish Education:
the Universities of Scotland." Scottish Nation 1 (April 1914):
87-88.

   An early article on a recurrent theme: the funding and
   control of the Scottish universities by English agencies.
   Donaldson argues that Scottish culture will suffer from
   this control.

58. Erskine, Ruaridh. "The British Superstition." Liberty 1
(October 2, 1920): 4.

   Erskine attacks the term "British" as racially and
   historically inaccurate, and suggests that it is
   unfair to Scots and English alike.

59. Erskine, Ruaridh. "The British Superstition." Liberty 1
(October 9, 1920): 117.

   Further arguments against the use of the term "British."

60. Erskine, Ruaridh. "The British Superstition." <u>Liberty</u>
1 (October 16, 1920): 1.

    Erskine argues against using "British" to describe
    events before the Union of 1707.

61. Erskine, Ruaridh. "The British Superstition." <u>Liberty</u> 1
(October 23, 1920): 1.

    The conclusion of Erskine's analysis of "British" and
    the term's inaccuracy. He offers more accurate terms to
    describe the English, Welsh, and Scots.

62. Erskine, Ruaridh. "Independence and Isolation." <u>Liberty</u>
2 (August 1921): 120.

    A thorough consideration of the forms, possibilities,
    and desirability of Scottish independence.

63. Erskine, Ruaridh. "Race and Culture." <u>Pictish Review</u>
1 (February 1928): 40-41.

    A defense of Scotland's right to cultural independence.
    Erskine concludes: it is the "mind and soul that make
    the nation", not size or political status.

64. Erskine, Ruaridh. "Unrealities." <u>Modern Scot</u> 1 (1930):
29-33.

    Erskine believes the political move for independence
    began with Home Rule for Ireland but concludes that the
    Gaelic Association in Scotland was more potent than any
    similar Irish organization. He hopes for a more radical
    approach to Scottish independence in the future.

65. Ferguson, R. Monro. "Reasons Why Scotland Should Have
Home Rule." <u>The Scottish Nation</u> 1 (December 1913): 25-27.

    Ferguson notes a blatant disregard in Parliament for
    Scottish business. He also demands immediate and radical
    agrarian reform.

66. Gibson, T. "The Reasons for a National Party." <u>Scots
Independent</u> (November 1927): 5.

    The need for a progressive party that would supplant the
    British parties. Many nationalists like Gibson were urging
    a national parliamentary party for Scotland at this time.

67. Gillies, Iain. "Scotland's Need: a National Party."
<u>Scots Independent</u> (September 1927): 7-10.

    A plea for a national party for Scotland in the year
    before that goal was achieved.

68. Gillies, Iain. "William Gillies: A Pioneer of Scots Nationalism." Scots Independent (September 1932): 166.

A summary of Gillies' political career, including his involvement with the Highland Land League, The Gaelic Society, and Irish Home Rule.

69. Gregory, J. "Scotland in the World." Scots Independent (December 1933): 23.

Gregory anticipates Scotland's role in the next war. He believes Scotland should gain independence before the war in order to insure neutrality.

70. Hogge, J.M. "A Human Document from the Highlands." The Scottish Nation 1 (November 1913): 7-8.

The Highlands are not romantic, writes Hogge, but are beset by deprivation of the worst sort. He argues that Home Rule is the only hope for the Highlands.

71. Hogge, J.M. "Scottish Nationality." The Scottish Nation 1 (February 1914): 57-58.

Why Home Rule is an urgent necessity for the Scottish Highlands.

72. Hogge, J.M. "Scots Home Rule: the Argument Stated." The Scottish Nation 1 (March 1914): 74.

Hogge compares the inefficiency of the modern British Parliament with the efficiency of the old Scottish Parliament.

73. Hogge, J.M. "Scots Home Rule-The Argument Stated: The Slur of Imperial Parliament." The Scottish Nation 1 (April 1914): 90.

Hogge, himself a Member of Parliament, comments on the delays in Parliament on Scottish business, resulting in much suffering and neglect in Scotland.

74. Hogge, J.M. "Scots Home Rule-The Argument Stated: Bleeding at the Pores." The Scottish Nation 1 (May 1914): 106.

Despite forced emigration and hunger, Hogge notes that 1/5 of Scotland's land is used for sport. He sees agrarian reform as Scotland's greatest need under Home Rule.

75. Hogge, J.M. "Scots Home Rule-The Argument Stated: Step by Step." The Scottish Nation 1 (June 1914): 126.

Hogge believes that the creation of the Secretary of State for Scotland in 1885 should accelerate Home Rule.

76. Hogge, J.M. "Scots Home Rule-The Argument Stated: 5."
The Scottish Nation 1 (July 1914): 135-136.

The impracticalities of conducting Scottish business
in a London Parliament.

77. Hogge, J.M. "Scots Home Rule-The Argument Stated: 6."
The Scottish Nation 1 (August 1914): 151.

Hogge comments that land reform will not come about in
the Highlands as long as so many English Members of
Parliament remain addicted to grouse and deer hunting.

78. Hogge, J.M. "Scots Home Rule-The Argument Stated: 7."
The Scottish Nation 1 (September 1914): 165.

Hogge uses the Scottish Small Landholders Act of 1911
as an example of Parliamentary injustice and incompetence
with regard to Scottish affairs.

79. Hogge, J.M. "Scots Home Rule-The Argument Stated: 8."
The Scottish Nation 1 (October 1914): 182.

Hogge concludes his series by noting the hypocrisy of
fighting for the rights of small nations while denying
them representation in Parliament.

80. Kerr, Lennox. "Literature: Class or National?" Outlook
(June 1936): 74-80.

Kerr argues that art is governed by class and that Scots
writers and artists should have nothing to do with
nationalism.

81. Lamont, Archie. "Marathon and Bannockburn: Towards
a Philosophy of Nationalism." Scots Independent (October 1934)
188-189.

Modern nationalism is seen by Lamont as a revival of the
Greek concept of balance and proportion.

82. Lamont, Norman. "The Case for Scottish Home Rule."
The Scottish Nation 1 (February 1914): 55-57.

Inadequate discussion of purely Scottish affairs in a
congested Parliament and the success of Federalism in
other nations are two major reasons offered by Lamont
for adoption of Home Rule for Scotland.

83. Lang, Ian. "Scots Home Rule in 1913: A Review of the
Year." The Scottish Nation 1 (February 1914): 50-51.

Lang summarizes legislation proposing Home Rule for
Scotland during 1913.

84. MacArthur, John. "Five Parliaments in One." Liberty 1 (April 1920): 33-34.

MacArthur recommends separate Parliaments for Britain's major divisions, thus ending congestion in Westminster.

85. MacArthur, John. "Self-Government for Scotland: What it Means." Liberty 1 (January 1920): 13-14.

A summary of the work done by the old Scottish Parliament, and how a new Scottish Parliament might model itself on that one.

86. MacArthur, John. "Why Scotland Needs a Divorce." Liberty 1 (October 9, 1920): 113-114.

The Union of 1707 is compared to a marriage that has gone stale due to what MacArthur terms "incompatability of temperament."

87. MacColl, Malcolm. "Commonsense for Clydeside Comrades." Scots Independent (September 1927): 1-2.

An appeal to halt the economic decline in Scotland by demanding immediate self-government with a socialist base.

88. MacCormick, John. "The Dawn of a New Era: Why You Should Vote Scottish Nationalist." Scottish Standard 1 (November 1935): 14.

MacCormick explains the advantages of voting for Scottish Nationalist candidates instead of the major British party candidates.

89. MacCormick, John. "The Next Step Forward." Scots Independent (February 1934): 1.

MacCormick sees the union of the Scottish Party with the National Party as a great move toward independence for Scotland.

90. MacCormick, John. "Youth and the National Party: Away with Waste and Poverty." Scots Independent (September 1928): 158-159.

Poor housing, high unemployment, rural decay, and other major problems facing Scotland can be solved only by self-government argues MacCormick.

91. MacDonald, J. "Home Rule and the Trade Unions." Scots Independent (December 1937): 7.

MacDonald challenges Scots to end English control over their trade unions and to organize more democratic ones.

92. MacDonnell, Joseph. "Labour's Unredeemed Pledges: Tom Johnston's Potato Bubble." Scots Independent (April 1930): 69-70.

A criticism of Tom Johnston's Development Board and its inability to solve Scotland's economic problems.

93. MacEwen, Sir Alexander. "Thoughts on the Election-and After." Scottish Standard 1(January 1936): 5-6.

MacEwen says the Scottish National Party should broaden its policies and welcome alliances with other groups. It should also attack economic problems without ignoring cultural ones.

94. MacEwen, Sir Alexander. "What Scottish National M.P.'s Can do for the Highlands and Islands." Scottish Standard 1 (November 1935): 13.

Explains his own candidacy as a Scottish Nationalist. Even lacking self-rule, MacEwen argues that even a few Scottish Nationalist M.P.'s could influence legislation that could halt the serious decay of the Highlands.

95. McGill, Alexander. "The American Union: a Lesson for the Home Rulers." Liberty 1 (November 20, 1920): 189-192.

Home Rulers often favor federation and McGill here discusses the American system, its strong and weak points, and the limits of its use as a model for Scottish Home Rule.

96. MacGille, Iosa Liam. "John MacLean and the Crown." Liberty 2 (June 1921): 83.

A criticism of the forces and laws that resulted in the imprisonment of the Scottish socialist John MacLean for his position against Scottish involvement in World War I.

97. MacKay, David N. "Advantages to Highlands of a Scottish Parliament." Scottish Home Rule Association News-Sheet 3 (November 1922): 30.

Article on how a Scottish Parliament would result in more participation by Highlanders in government and bring democracy to where it had never been before.

98. Mackenzie, Compton. "Creative Nationalism." Scots Independent (March 1932): 72.

The famous address given at Mackenzie's installation as Lord Rector of Glasgow University, Jan. 29, 1932. This famous address called for nationalists to be more daring and creative, and to use Scottish Nationalism as a liberating force.

99.   Mackenzie, Compton. "The National Party." Modern Scot
1 (Winter 1931): 25-29.

Here, Mackenzie argues for the independence of the
National Party and warns of the dangers of merger or
compromise.

100.   Mackenzie, Compton. "R.B. Cunninghame Graham: Scottish
Nationalist." Outlook (May 1936): 21-24.

A eulogy on the death of Cunninghame Graham and a
tribute to his political contributions.

101.   Mackenzie, Compton. "Towards a Scottish Idea." Pictish
Review 1 (February 1928): 40.

This article observes that nationalism is not a
territorial concept. It praises C.M. Grieve's concept
of the "Scottish idea."

102.   Mackenzie, Compton. "What's Wrong with Scotland?"
Scots Independent (December 1929): 19-21.

A diatribe against what Mackenzie sees as the more mer-
cenary and narrow aspects of the Scottish character.

103.   Macneacail, H.C. "What is a Scot?" Scots Independent
(May 1927): 8-10.

An attempt to sort out Scotland's racial and linguistic
elements, concluding that Scotland is essentially
Celtic, both Highland and Lowland.

104.   MacPherson, Hector. "The Evolution of Scottish
Nationalism." The Scottish Nation 1 (December 1913): 24-25

Scotland's separate legal and education systems are
seen as the two key factors in the struggle for
independence.

105.   MacPherson, Hector. "The Scottish National Movement."
The Scottish Nation 1 (November 1913): 2-3.

A review of the many Scottish Home Rule Bills up to 1913.

106.   MacPherson, Hector. "Tory Opposition to Scottish Home
Rule." The Scottish Nation 1 (June 1914): 116-117.

Why the Tories can never support Home Rule for Scotland.

107.   Maxwell, Stuart. "Perth: Capital of Scotland." Scots
Independent (April 1932): 87.

Reasons in support of Perth's claim to be the future
capital of an independent Scotland.

108.   Muir, Edwin. "Pages from a Scottish Journey." Modern
Scot 6 (Spring 1935): 18-28.

In Part II, Muir explains how only Socialism or Communism
can cure Scotland's material and spiritual problems.
Muir also believes that Scotland's nationalists are too
feeble and unimaginative to bring about change. He
concludes this famous essay with the hope for "100 years
of Socialism."

109.   Muirhead, Roland. "Debate: a Nationalist Party."
Scottish Home Rule 6 (December 1925): 53.

A debate between Muirhead and David N. MacKay about the
desirability of forming a national party. Muirhead
argues that Home Rule would never result from the
policies of the major British parties, while MacKay
argues that no national party could ever succeed in
the polls.

110.   Muirhead,Roland. "A Scottish National Party?" Scottish
Home Rule 8 (February 1928): 197-198.

Muirhead answers questions about the need for a national
party for Scotland.

111.   Napier, Theodore. "Editorial." Fiery Cross (January
1907): 2.

Napier, an early nationalist, gives the reasons for
publishing the Fiery Cross, one of the most influential
early political journals in Scotland.

112.   Napier, Theodore. "Government of Scotland Bill."
Fiery Cross (October 1911): 5.

The excitement generated by a bill introduced in August,
1911, by Sir Henry Dalziel, to give Scotland its own
Parliament.

113.   Napier, Theodore. "Is There a Scottish Nation?"
Fiery Cross (January 1904): 3.

Scotland's separate legal and educational systems make
national independence more likely, writes Napier.

114.   Napier, Theodore. "Patriotism not Jingoism." Fiery
Cross (January 1904): 2-3.

Napier argues, as did almost all Irish Nationalists, that
the Boer War should serve as a warning to break all ties
with imperialist England. He urges Scots to oppose the
Boer War.

115. Napier, Theodore. "The Scottish National League."
Fiery Cross (October 1904): 2-3.

   The newly-formed League's aims are explained, including
   its plan to bring forward national candidates and to
   campaign for a Scottish Parliament.

116. Napier, Theodore. "A Scottish National Party." Fiery
Cross (July 1903): 2.

   A call for a party in Scotland that can duplicate
   Parnell's successes in Ireland. Napier's goal: self-
   government within federation.

117. Napier, Theodore. "The Young Scots Society." Fiery
Cross (October 1907): 7.

   Praises the Young Scots Society and its goal of a
   Scottish Parliament.

118. Ponsonby, A.W. "Scotland and Federalism." The Scottish
Nation 1 (June 1914): 117-118.

   Why Scotland should begin preparing for Home Rule under
   a federal system. Ponsonby reminds the English that
   Home Rule for Scotland also means Home Rule for England,
   thus England's politicians should plan accordingly.

119. Power, William. "Has the Scots Literary Renaissance
Arrived?" Scots Independent (August 1931): 148.

   Power notes Scotland's cultural awakening, but doubts
   that Scotland can support its artists and writers.

120. Power, William. "The Real Curse of Scotland." Scottish
Standard 1 (March 1935): 7-8.

   Power argues that Scotland's tragedy was the cultural
   break with Europe in the 17th century, resulting in
   introversion and conservatism. Nationalists should
   reverse this process by making Scotland part of
   European culture once more.

121. Ruskin, John. "Letter." Fiery Cross (April 1905): 3.

   A reprint of Ruskin's letter first appearing on Jan. 16,
   1887, in the Pall Mall Gazette, in which he explained
   his support for Home Rule movements in Britain.

122. Ryswick, Charles. "Those Warriors of Scotland: the Tale
of a Few Dozen Sheep," Scottish Standard 1 (July 1935): 16-17.

   A strong criticism of Scotland's current Members of
   Parliament. Ryswick hopes that Home Rule might produce
   men of more integrity.

123. Scottish Home Rule Association. "Three Home Rule
Schemes." Scottish Home Rule Association News Sheet 3
(September 1922): 2.

   Compares the two Scottish Home Rule Bills of 1922, with
   the Constitution of the Irish Free State.

124. Spence, Lewis. "A Great Year for Scotland." Scots
Independent (February 1930): 41.

   Spence concludes that 1929 was a good year, having
   resulted in cultural and political rebirth for Scotland.

125. Spence, Lewis. "The Meaning of Patriotism: its Self
Analysis." Scots Independent (December 1930): 21.

   An anthropologist's view of nationalism as a means to
   preserve a valuable culture and to prevent racial
   extinction.

126. Spence, Lewis. "The Scots National League Convention
Appeal." The Scottish Nation 1 (June 19, 1923): 14.

   An outline of the views of the Scots National League.

127. Spence, Lewis. "The Survival of the Scot." Scots
Independent (March 1931): 72.

   Another expression of Spence's conviction that nations,
   like species, can become extinct. He sees Scottish
   survival as dependent on self-government.

128. Spence, Lewis. "Whither Scottish Nationalism: Present
Chaos and Future Order." Scots Independent (April 1929):
65-66.

   Spence is concerned about the divisions in Scotland
   between Gaelic and English, Highland and Lowland,
   Royalist and Socialist, Protestant and Catholic, etc.
   He asks Scottish Nationalists to avoid extremes,
   practice tolerance, and shed some of the ancient
   Scottish prejudices.

129. Spence, Rhoda. "Women and Scottish Nationalism."
Scots Independent (February 1929): 41.

   The harsh realities have forced Scots women to be
   strong and durable. Economic freedom for Scotland should
   end their exploitation. Spence hopes that Scottish
   Nationalism will liberate women and men alike.

130. Torrence, John. "Freedom in Politics: the Party that
Scotland Wants." Outlook (May 1936): 39-42.

   Criticism of the National Party for its austerity and
   remoteness from the people.

131. Waddie, Charles. "How the English Parties Treat
Scotland." The Thistle 2 (January 1910): 13-15.

  After fifty years in politics, Waddie concludes that no
  national British party can achieve Home Rule for
  Scotland. He concludes that only a Scottish party can
  achieve that.

132. Waddie, Charles. "The Young Scots Society and Home
Rule for Scotland." The Scottish Nationalist 1 (June 1903):

  A report of the annual meeting of the Young Scots
  Society, held in Edinburgh on June 16, 1903, in
  support of Home Rule.

133. Wanliss, T. "The Scottish Home Rule Manifesto."
The Thistle 1 (June 1909): 165-169.

  Wanliss concludes that the Liberal Party will never
  bring Home Rule to Scotland. His argument foreshadows
  the creation of the national parties in Scotland,
  particularly, the Scottish National Party.

134. Wanliss, T."The Young Scots Society and Home Rule."
The Thistle 1 (November 1909): 244-245.

  Comments on the significance of The Young Scots Society's
  criticism of the Liberal Party's inability to bring
  about Home Rule. There was much talk at this time of the
  formation of national Parliamentary parties for Scotland.

135. Whyte, A.F. "Scots Home Rule and the American Union:
a False Analogy." The Scottish Nation 1 (July 1914): 138.

  Scots should not initiate federalism on American lines,
  says Whyte, because of the very different historical
  circumstance. A strong criticism of the federal idea,
  long popular with Scottish Nationalists, and a key
  part of the Liberal Party's idea on Scottish Home Rule.

136. Whyte, J.H. "The Background of Present-Day Nationalism:
1." Modern Scot 2 (Winter 1932): 266-269.

  Nationalism should be a means to preserve and attain
  culture and should never be based on race, religion, or
  language solely, argues Whyte. He cautions against
  abuses of nationalism, citing Hitler as an example.

137. Whyte, J.H. "The Background of Present-Day Nationalism:
II." Modern Scot 3 (April 1932): 4-8.

  He traces the national idea from antiquity and labels it
  a "vital force." Cautions against aberrations of
  nationalism.

138. Whyte, J.H. "The Background of Present-Day Nationalism:
III." Modern Scot 3 (Summer 1932): 92-97.

Presents an ideal of a "free individual" with a truly
European identity of Scotland in Europe.

139. Whyte, J.H. "The Catholic Irish in Scotland." Modern
Scot 5 (Winter 1935): 222-229.

The Irish in Scotland as a political factor. The
Scottish National Party should not pander to either the
protestant or catholic vote in Scotland, but must ensure
religious liberty for all.

140. Whyte, J.H. "Nationalism and the Artist." Modern Scot
3 (November 1932): 282-286.

If art is universal, asks Whyte, can a Scottish Nationalist be a true artist? Yes, he answers, if that nationalism
is part of a creative and international culture. Whyte
argues here, as many nationalists have done, that
small nations, because they can't be economically
self-sufficient, must be international in outlook in
order to survive as small nations.

141. Whyte, J.H. "The Political Future." Modern Scot 5
(October 1934): 136-140.

To date, says Whyte, Scottish Nationalists have failed
because they haven't convinced people of their aims and
of their sincerity.

142. Whyte, J.H. "Scottish Nationalism." Modern Scot 4
(April 1933): 4-11.

Whyte sees Scotland as a very complex culture and
cautions nationalists and others to avoid simple
solutions to Scotland's problems. Also, he questions
whether political solutions can produce altered
states of awareness.

143. Whyte, J.H. "Scottish Nationalism -II." Modern Scot 4
(Summer 1933): 94-99.

Contrasts Scottish Nationalism with Nazism. He also
attacks the Scottish Fascist Democratic Party ("blue
shirts") for their racist policies.

144. Whyte, J.H. "Scottish Nationalism-III." Modern Scot 4
(Autumn 1933): 178-184.

A discussion of Scottish education and literature and
how Scottish students suffer under a grant system
that favors English students and English culture.

145.   Whyte, J.H. "Scottish Nationalism IV: Highlands and Lowlands." _Modern Scot_ 4 (January 1934): 270-276.

Whyte surveys the Highland/Lowland "problem" and believes that Scottish regeneration can only come about through a harmony of both. "Celtic revival" is not the answer, but rather a renewal of "communal life".

146.   Wilson, John. "Empire, Nationalism, and Federation." _The Scottish Patriot_ (April 1905): 72-75.

Wilson argues that true federation must be based on equality. He cites Canada and South Africa as examples.

146a.   Wilson, John. "The Programme of the Scottish National League." _The Scottish Patriot_ (July 1904): 82.

The aims of the Scottish National League, founded in May, 1904.

3.

1940–1959: TROUBLED SLEEP

The Scottish National Party denies the legal or moral right
of the British or any other alien government to conscript
Scots men and women for any purpose.
                                    Scottish National Party
                                    Conference Resolution
                                    June, 1944

World War II brought active opposition from Scots nationalists
and socialists, many of whom went to prison for their anti-
war activities. Differences between anti-war militants and
pro-war moderates resulted in a major defection from the
Scottish National Party in 1942, with the creation of
John MacCormick's Scottish Convention. Meanwhile, Robert
McIntyre won a nationalist seat in the historic Motherwell
by-election of 1945. During these decades, Scottish
Nationalism had more sympathy than votes, but the daring
capture of the Stone of Scone, the ancient coronation stone
of Scotland, from Westminster in 1950, revealed broad
popular support for Scottish Nationalism. At this time,
the Scottish Convention circulated the "Scottish Covenant",
a petition calling for a Scottish Parliament. The petition
claimed an incredible $2\frac{1}{2}$ million signatures within two
years of its appearance in 1949. Leading intellectuals
and writers like Neil Gunn, Hugh MacDiarmid, Naomi Mitchison
and others urged more creative socialist and radical policies,
and called for a more militant approach to Scotland's
cultural problems. The apparent calm and security of post-
war Scotland may have been preparation for the in-fighting
to follow. None could foresee the convincing electoral
victories of the Scottish Nationalists in the 1970's.

BOOKS AND PAMPHLETS

147.   Barr, James. Lang Syne. Glasgow: Maclellan, 1949. 384 pp.

Barr (1862-1949) was a Free Church minister with long
involvement with civil and religious rights. He was also
a member of the Independent Labour Party and served as
Member of Parliament. He was a pacifist and nationalist,
serving as chairman of the influential London Scottish
Self-Government Committee. A biography of an incredible
career.

148.   Brown, Oliver. Scotland-Nation or Desert? Glasgow:
Scottish Socialist Party, 1944. 48pp.

Dedicated to Douglas Young, Scots Nationalist imprisoned
for his opposition to WWII. Anecdotal, employing press
clippings and popular quotes. Brown was a leading
socialist and nationalist and editor of the Scots
Socialist. His aim: "A free socialist Scotland."
Brown uses much humor and whimsy to reveal Scotland's
need for independence from England.

149.   Brown, Oliver. Scotlandshire: England's Worst-Governed
Province. Glasgow: Scottish National Party, 1945. 48pp.

Pamphlet containing quotes, articles, extractions,
showing Scotland's need for self-government. Brown
concentrates on infant mortality, poor housing, and the
decline of Scottish industry.

150.   Burns, Thomas. "Giving Government Back to the Scottish
People." In The New Scotland, by the London Scots Self-
Government Committee, 13-29. Glasgow: Civic Press, 1943.

A broad discussion on features of a self-governing
Scotland, including local self-government and parish
self-government, the functions of a restored Scots
Parliament. Concludes that a democratic Scotland could
serve as a model and leader in the world community of
smaller nations.

151.   Coupland, Sir Reginald. Welsh and Scottish Nationalism:
a Study.London: Collins, 1954. 426pp.

Coupland devotes his book to a study of Welsh and Scots
Home Rule movements since the 17th century, having
studied nationalism in Canada, Palestine, West Africa,
and South Africa. He sees dangers in both separatism
and unity. An objective study, he believes in more
autonomy and devolution in the British Isles. Local
parliaments may be a solution.

152. Evans, Gwynfor. <u>Our Three Nations</u>. Cardiff: Plaid
Cymru, 1956. 79pp.

Welsh, Scottish, and English nationalism are surveyed.
The author believes that freedom for Scotland and Wales
will mean true democracy for England as well. A
"confraternity" of these nations should be the goal.

153. Gibb, Andrew Dewar. <u>Scotland Resurgent</u>. Stirling:
Eneas MacKay, 1950. 308pp.

For Gibb, World War II proved the failing of large
nations. Small nations such as Scotland can insure peace,
prosperity, and international co-operation. Nationalism
is neutral, and can be used for good or ill, thus, notes
Gibb, the nationalism of large nations should be suspect.

154. Hamilton, Ian R. <u>No Stone Unturned</u>. London: Gollancz,
1952. 191pp.

An account of the removal of the famed Stone of Scone
from Westminster Abbey by Scottish nationalists, among
them the author. The stone, according to tradition, was
used at the coronations of Scottish kings. The symbolism
of this act is discussed throughout the book.

155. Johnston, Thomas. <u>Memories</u>. London: Collins, 1952.
255pp.

Memoirs of the famous Secretary of State for Scotland.
Chapter 9, "A Nation Once Again", is useful for the student
of nationalism, and his personal sketches of Roland
Muirhead, James Connolly, and James Barr give valuable
insights into Scottish politics.

156. Kohn, Hans. <u>The Idea of Nationalism: a Study in its
Origins and Background</u>. NY: Macmillan, 1946. 735pp.

Kohn traces the concept of nationalism through Israel,
Greece, and Rome to modern states, and explains its
philosophical and political basis.

157. Kohr, Leopold. <u>The Breakdown of Nations</u>. London: Kegan
Paul, 1957. 244pp.

Theories on the size of the ideal state. Cultural,
economic, administrative, and philosophical arguments
for small nations. Examples of successful and
unsuccessful federation are given.

158. Lamont, Archie. Scotland and War. Glasgow: Scots
Secretariat, 1943. 32pp.

   Lamont's defense before a tribunal on Sept. 1942 in
   Birmingham, for resisting conscription. Lamont, as a
   conscientious objector, believed that large nations are
   necessarily imperialist and war-provoking, at the
   expense both of world peace and democracy. In general,
   his defense is a plea for a world of small, self-
   governing nations.

159. Lamont, Archie. Scottish Neutrality: Disarmament Means
Prosperity. Glasgow: The Scots Secretariat, 1949. 40pp.

   The constitutional and legal objections of Scottish
   Nationalists to conscription in World War II are
   presented. The rights of small nations are identified.
   The concepts of "passive neutrality" and "non-violent .
   non-cooperation" are defended.

160. London Scots Self-Government Committee. The New Scotland.
Glasgow: Civic Press, 1943. 178pp.

   Seventeen chapters on science, raw materials, architecture,
   banking, agriculture, fishing, arts and legal reform are
   presented within the possibilities of a future, self-
   governing Scotland.

161. MacCormick, John M. The Flag in the Wind: the Story of
the National Movement in Scotland. London: Gollancz, Ltd.
1955. 222pp.

   Autobiography. MacCormick traces his involvement with
   nationalist politics from his days as a law student at
   Glasgow University. Important material on the National
   Party, the Scottish Covenant, the Neutrality League, etc.
   A list of important individuals in the Scottish political
   and cultural renaissance. Covers 1923-1954.

162. MacCormick, John. Scottish Convention. Glasgow:
Maclellan, 1943. 44pp.

   Explains the purpose of the Scottish Convention, founded
   to bring together all parties and people who desire an
   independent Scotland.

163. MacCormick, John M. Scottish Convention: an Experiment
in Democracy. Glasgow: Maclellan, 1943. 44pp.

   MacCormick discusses the origin, name, and purpose of the
   Scottish Convention, which he founded in Glasgow in
   June, 1942. The Convention resulted after disagreement
   within Scottish National Party ranks.

164. MacIntosh, Sandy. 100 Home Rule Questions. Dundee:
Graham's Advertising Service, 1949. 81pp.

An SNP member answers one hundred of the most common
questions and criticisms of Scottish Nationalism. The
questions range from the theoretical to the practical.
The answers are not official SNP policy.

165. Mann, Jean. "Scotland Tomorrow Lost Horizons." In
The New Scotland, by the London Scots Self-Government
Committee, 163-168. Glasgow: Civic Press, 1943.

Discusses problems of industry, education, and housing
and how a Scottish Socialist government can end major
problems such as emigration and slums.

166. The Scottish Convention. Hansard on Scotland: An
Account of a Remarkable Debate. Glasgow: Maclellan, 1942.
63pp.

An account of an important debate on Scottish affairs,
which took place in the House of Commons on May 12,1942,
in which Tom Johnston, Secretary of State for Scotland
and others urged a strong post-war remedy for Scotland,
and recommended autonomy.

167. Turner, Arthur C. Scottish Home Rule. Oxford: Blackwell,
1952. 76pp.

Turner examines Scottish Home Rule movements before 1939
and compares them with movements after 1939. He studies
the economic causes that generate feelings for Home Rule.
Concludes that successful self-government must have a
strong economic base.

168. Young, Douglas. Labour Record on Scotland. Glasgow:
Scots Secretariat, 1949. 23pp.

An address on Dec. 16, 1948,by Douglas Young to the
Aberdeen Branch of Scottish Universities Labour Party.
A description of the relationship between Home Rule and
the Labour Party, with an indictment of the many Labour
promises that have been broken with regard to Home Rule
in Scotland.

ARTICLES

169. Britton, Robert. "The Future of the National Movement
in Scotland." Forum 1 (August 1946): 4-5.

A call for a "united front" of all individuals and
groups desiring independence for Scotland.

170.   Brown, Oliver. "The British Gestapo." <u>Scots Socialist</u>
(1949): 3.

Brown recounts the intimidation of Scottish socialists
during World War II, paying special attention to the
arrest of the Scottish Nationalist and journalist,
Arthur Donaldson, in June, 1940. Brown's own editorial
offices of the <u>Scots Socialist</u> were raided by the
police at the outbreak of the war.

171.   Brown, Oliver. "Cranks and Nationalism." <u>National
Weekly</u> 4 (July 5, 1952): 3.

Diatribe against Scottish National Party conservatives
by a leading Scottish journalist.

172.   Brown, Oliver. "Douglas Young and Scotland."
<u>National Weekly</u> 4 (August 2, 1952): 2.

A criticism of what Brown believes are contradictions
in Douglas Young's Scottish Nationalism.

173.   Brown, Oliver. "Douglas Young and the Way to Freedom."
<u>National Weekly</u> 4 (Jan. 12, 1952): 1.

A rebuttal to Douglas Young's claim that the Labour
Party is the best vehicle for Scottish independence.

174.   Brown, Oliver. "John MacCormick." <u>National Weekly</u> 2
(Jan. 7, 1950): 2.

Comments on the return of John MacCormick to active
Scottish Nationalism with the launching of his
Covenant movement. Brown reviews MacCormick's
successes and failures over the years, and tries to
evaluate MacCormick's political worth.

175.   Brown, Oliver. "The National Movement: What Now?"
<u>National Weekly</u> 4 (Oct. 6, 1951): 3.

A call for unity among the supporters of Scots
independence, with the need to harness what Brown finds
as overwhelming grassroots support for Home Rule.

176.   Brown, Oliver. "The Scottish National Party: A Record
of Twenty-One Years." <u>National Weekly</u> 1 (July 2, 1949): 5.

An assessment of the record of the Scottish National
Party. Brown concludes: "In spite of its obvious
blunders and weaknesses, it has justified its existence."

177.   Brown, Oliver. "The State of Scottish Nationalism."
<u>National Weekly</u> 5 (Feb. 14, 1953): 1.

Despite its electoral failures, Brown finds much
sympathy in Scotland for Home Rule.

178. Brown, Oliver. "The Unionist Party and the Question of Self-Government." National Weekly 4 (Nov. 27, 1951): 1.

Brown points out inconsistencies in the Unionist Party's historical support for Home Rule.

179. Brown, Oliver. "The Value of Violence." National Weekly 5 (Jan. 24, 1953): 1.

Drawing lessons from Ireland and India, Brown finds that violence can achieve political ends, but also finds that "non-cooperation" is equally effective.

180. Brown, Oliver. "The Verdict of Some Foreigners on Scottish Nationalism." National Weekly 3 (Sept. 8, 1951): 2-3.

Brown reviews the opinions of some French intellectuals who support Home Rule for Scotland.

181. Brown, Oliver. "We Defend the Irish." Scots Socialist (1947): 1.

While acknowledging its many problems, Brown supports the Irish Republic and its policies since independence.

182. Brown, Oliver. "Where Does the National Party Come In?" National Weekly 2 (Dec. 10, 1949): 5.

Brown questions the need for the frequent and harmful purges and divisions within the ranks of Scottish Nationalism.

183. Brown, Oliver. "Whited Sepulchres." Scots Socialist (1957): 4.

Brown brands the church in Scotland as the biggest barrier to political and cultural freedom in Scotland.

184. Douglas, C.H. "Economic and Financial Reconstruction: Draft Social Credit Scheme for Scotland 1933 and 1945." National Weekly 3 (March 24, 1951): 3.

A ten-point method on the best way to implement Social Credit in Scotland, by the Scottish founder of the Social Credit idea. Social Credit was favored by many intellectuals in the 1930's and 1940's, including Ezra Pound and Hugh MacDiarmid.

185. Drysdale, C. Douglas. "The Truth Will Out." Catalyst (Dec. 1967): 18-19.

Drysdale believes that Scotland's post World War II life has been so disastrous that no possible reason can exist for continued alliance with England.

186. Duke of Montrose. "Self Government for Scotland."
Today and Tomorrow 1 (Spring 1946): 7-10.

   Arguments for "a responsible democratic legislative
   assembly." Divides powers into "domestic" (health,
   housing, and education) vs. "reserved" (defense, foreign
   affairs, etc.).

187. Durness, John. "A Chiel Amang Ye." Scots Review 7
(Feb. 1947): 5.

   Durness lists the key divisions in the nationalist ranks:
   left vs. right, separation vs. devolution, and a major
   one: state planning vs. private planning.

188. Erskine, Ruaridh. "Celtic Reappearances." National
Weekly 2 (Dec. 3, 1949): 5.

   Erskine challenges the teaching of Scottish history in
   the schools and proposes several remedies, including
   his own pamphlets which stress Irish connections and
   Celtic traditions and politics.

189. Ferguson, Duncan. "Scotland's Political Untouchables."
Scots Review 10 (July 1949); 66-67.

   Ferguson calls Scottish Nationalists the "gadflies of
   Scottish politics" whose influence is greater than
   election results would indicate.

190. Gibson, J.M. "Home Rule and the History Books." Forum
1 (August 1947): 10-11.

   How early education and teaching may have been a
   negative influence on the Scottish masses and how
   Scotland's cautious approach to self-rule might be
   changed by a more dynamic method of teaching history.

191. Gibson, T.H. "The Scottish Political Movement-Part I."
Scots Independent (December 1951): 8.

   Traces the history of the Young Scots Society and its
   influence on Home Rule within the Liberal and Labour
   Parties.

192. Gibson, T.H. "The Scottish Political Movement." Scots
Independent (February 1952): 8-9.

   The Liberal Party, its history with Scottish Home Rule,
   and its inability to accommodate true Scots radicalism
   in the form of the Land League.

193. Gibson, T.H. "The Scottish Political Movement-Part IV."
Scots Independent (June 1952): 10.

   Traces Home Rule ideas in the Liberal Party and the
   adoption of those ideas by the Labour Party.

194. Gibson, T.H. "The Scottish Political Movement-Part IV,
Continued." Scots Independent (July 1952): 13-14.

   Discusses James Maxton, James Barr, Tom Johnston, John
   Wheatley, Manny Shinwell and other radicals who
   believed that a London-based Labour Party could not
   adopt proper policies for Scotland.

195. Gibson, T.H. "The Scottish Political Movement-V."
Scots Independent (September 1952): 8-9.

   Discusses the historical failures of the major political
   parties to solve Scotland's critical social problems in
   health and housing.

196. Gibson, T.H. "The Scottish Political Movement-Part VI."
Scots Independent (November 1952): 7-8.

   Useful first-hand account of events surrounding the
   founding of the National Party in 1928. Gives
   important information on the roles played by Spence,
   MacCormick, and others.

197. Gibson, T,H. "The Scottish Political Movement-VIII."
Scots Independent (June 1953): 5-6.

   Gibson outlines lessons for Scotland from Irish Home
   Rule. He believes the discipline of Parnell's
   Parliamentary party should be carefully studied by
   Scottish Nationalists.

198. Gilmour, B. "Blueprint for Scotland." Scottish Journal
(Christmas 1952): 6.

   Instead of a separate Parliament, Gilmour envisions a
   more workable system of local governmental units with
   the creation of Departments of Fuel, Power, Transport, etc.

199. Gunn, Neil. "Sir Alexander MacEwen: Philosopher,
Patriot and Beloved Leader." Scots Independent (August 1941):
7.

   A memorial and tribute to Sir Alexander MacEwen by
   a leading Scottish novelist.

200. Gunn, Neil. "Why Are Writers Nationalists?" Scots
Independent (November 1940): 7.

Gunn, a major Scottish novelist, states the view that
a writer's nation and culture can't be denied without
severe emotional or psychological damage to the writer
and his art. Gunn believes that Scottish writers have
much at stake in Scotland's struggles for independence.

201. Hamilton, Iain. "Nationalism in Music." Scottish
Journal (May/June 1953): 12-13.

Hamilton remarks on the influence of nationalism on
Chopin, Moussorgsky, Smetana, Dvorak, and others,
and wonders why Scotland has yet to produce composers of
similar stature, despite Scotland's rich folk culture.

202. Henderson, Hamish. "Scotland and the World Peace
Congress." National Weekly 1 (May 7, 1949): 2.

An important international conference held in Paris in
April of 1947. Henderson reports on the reception and
contribution of the Scottish contingent, giving rise
to speculation about an independent Scotland's possible
role in international affairs.

203. Irvine, G. Innes. "Scottish National Party Strengths
and Weakness." Scottish Journal (Feb. March 1953): 14.

Irvine lists the key weaknesses of the SNP: too much
emphasis on Gaelic, too little support for local
branches, and lack of cooperation among Scottish
Nationalists in general.

204. Lamont, Archie. "Charles Waddie: a Scottish Nationalist
Pioneer." National Weekly 2 (March 25, 1950): 2.

A sketch of Waddie's life as an early Home Ruler, editor,
and key nationalist figure in the late 19th and early
20th centuries.

205. Lamont, Archie. "Cunninghame Graham's Politics-1."
National Weekly 4 (Sept. 6, 1952): 3.

Early factors influencing Graham's later politics.

206. Lamont, Archie. "Cunninghame Graham's Politics. "
National Weekly 5 (Sept. 12, 1952): 4.

Concentrates on Graham's early involvement with
Scottish Nationalism in the 1886 Home Rule
Association.

207. Lamont, Archie. "A Scottish Neutrality Congress."
National Weekly 1 (June 11, 1949): 2.

An address by Hugh MacDiarmid and Oliver Brown on " A
Neutral Scottish Republic" in which neutrality is urged
for Scotland in the event of another war.

208. Law, T.S. "The Scotland I'd Like to See." New Scot 2
(December 1946): 24-26.

Law prefers what he calls a "republic of realization"
with the Scots language spoken throughout Scotland.

209. Lindsay, Maurice. "The Scotland I'd Like to See."
New Scot 3 (May 1947): 24-26.

A Scottish poet envisions a self-governing Scotland,
promoting its languages and culture. Lindsay argues also
for the disestablishment of the Church of Scotland,
which Lindsay says "has blighted the life of our people
for over 300 years."

210. Lindsay, Maurice. "The Winds of Change." Scots Review
11 (January 1951): 186.

Lindsay concludes that Scottish literature fares better
in 1951 than it has in the previous fifty years and
also notes how "an improved literary position is not
without its political aspect."

211. Loch, Norman. "Hypnotized Scots." Scots Independent
(February 1946): 3.

Loch, having lived in Canada, is dismayed by the
ignorance of Scottish affairs there. He feels that most
Scots abroad and their descendants seem to prefer
romantic versions of Scotland to the harsher realities.

212. MacCormick, John M. "A Covenant Summing-Up."
The Nationalist 2 (April 29, 1950): 1.

MacCormick writes on the significance of the two million
signatures to the Covenant, a petition asking Scots
to sign in support of Home Rule within federation.

213. MacCormick, John. "The Parties and the State- the
New Oligarchy." Scottish Journal (October 1952): 3.

A rationale for the Covenant Association and a criticism
of the corruption of the major political parties in
Britain.

214. Maccolla, Fionn. "The Scotland I'd Like to See."
New Scot 2 (April 1947): 24-26.

Maccolla (pseudonym for Tom MacDonald) novelist,
author of And the Cock Crew, would desire an
independent Scotland capable of solving the housing
and health problems, and capable of stimulating the
Gaelic language and the nation's culture generally.

215. McCallum, Neil. "Speaking of Myself." Scots Review 8
(June 1947): 35.

Scottish Nationalists should not dwell on the past,
but should prove their capacity to solve modern problems.

216. Macewen, David. "Scotland and the Covenant." Scots
Review 10 (December 1949): 160.

The Scottish Convention issued a "Covenant" in 1949,
supporting Home Rule in a federal Britain. This
covenant drew over $2\frac{1}{2}$ million signatures. Macewen and
others see in the support for the Covenant undeniable
proof to skeptics that the majority of Scots want some
measure of Home Rule.

217. MacInnes, Hector. "What is Wrong with Scottish
Nationalism?" The Lion Rampant 1 (1947): 34-35.

MacInnes criticizes Scottish Nationalism as being too
bland and phlegmatic. He says it should be buoyant
and adventurous instead.

218. McIntyre, Robert. "The Political and National
Alternative to Tory and Labour Unionism." Scottish Journal
(November 1952): 7.

A plan of action on how the Scottish National Party
can win support from Labour voters.

219. McIntyre, Robert. "Scotland Has Her Own Crisis: Solve
it First." Scots Independent (Feb. 1952): 1-2.

A blast at Tory incompetence in Scotland.

220. Mackenzie, Compton. "The Cunninghame Graham I Knew."
Scots Independent (July 1952): 7-8.

Mackenzie's tribute to a legendary politician and
writer.

221. MacKinnon, Iain. "Nationalism in Celtia." National
Weekly 4 (Feb. 23, 1952): 1.

Reports on movements for independence and cultural
revival in Wales, Man, Cornwall, and Brittany, and
the significance of these movements to Scotland.

222. McNeil, Clement. "The Attack on Identity." <u>New Alliance</u> 3 (April/May 1942): 4-5.

The effects of Scotland's loss of nationhood on the psychology of the individual Scot, by a psychiatrist.

223. McNeill, F. Marion. "Celtic Congress Resumes." <u>Scots Independent</u> (September 1947): 5.

After 8 years, a Celtic Congress was held once more, in Dublin in July, 1947, attended by representatives from Ireland, Wales, Brittany, Scotland, and Man. Sorley MacLean, the Scottish Gaelic poet, expressed his belief that only a sympathetic Home Rule government could save Gaelic in Scotland.

224. McOmish, Farquhar. "Nationalism: a View." <u>Scots Review</u> 8 (April 1947): 3.

The liquidation of the British Empire after World War II makes moderate nationalist opinion outdated. Scotland should imitate Burma and India, argues the writer, and negotiate immediately for independence.

225. Mitchison, Naomi. "The Union-Good and Bad." <u>Today and Tomorrow</u> 1 (Summer 1946): 31-35.

In retrospect, Mitchison believes the Union may have been necessary, but since those conditions no longer prevail, Scotland should develop a true nationalism and internationalism, no longer linked to England.

226. Muirhead, R.E. "Scots Wha Hae..." <u>Scots Review</u> 9 (Nov. 1948): 108.

A profile of Roland Eugene Muirhead and his role in the history of Scottish Nationalism.

227. Muirhead, R.E. "Why a Scottish National Congress." <u>National Weekly</u> 3 (Jan. 27, 1951): 1-2.

Sketch of Home Rule from 1852, with proof that the Scottish National Congress founded by Muirhead is the only possible way to obtain Home Rule.

228. Murray, David. "The Western Isles." <u>National Weekly</u> 4 (October 13, 1951): 3.

As a member of the Scottish Liberal Party and a supporter of Home Rule, Murray calls for his party to return to its "pure-root Radical Liberalism" which supported Irish and Scottish Home Rule in the past.

229. Porteous, James A. "A Free Society." Scots Review 11 (March 1951): 216.

Porteous writes of functional and territorial devolution, and sees democracy as a prerequisite for both.

230. Porteous, James A. "Home Rule and the Businessman." Scots Review 10 (February 1950): 204.

Businessmen should have no fears over an independent Scotland. Porteous argues that Scotland could be more prosperous than Norway or Sweden.

231. Porteous, James A. "Home Rule: Economic and Financial Effects." Scots Review 10 (March 1950): 222-223.

The article states how independence would bring increased trade with England and would lessen bureaucracy.

232. Porteous, James A. "Self Government and the Election." Today and Tomorrow 1 (Spring 1946): 33-35.

Considers typical arguments against Home Rule: its cost, lack of real power, etc. Porteous answers each argument in turn.

233. Power, William. "Community Life in Scotland." Today and Tomorrow 1 (Spring 1946): 21-25.

Power notes the strength of community life in Scotland. This communal life might be a positive influence on an independent Scotland.

234. Power, William. "Do We Deserve Home Rule?" Scots Independent (Feb. 1941): 3.

Power hopes that true political independence would result in total liberation in art, music, architecture, etc. He doubts that most Scots are prepared to handle change at this level.

235. Power, William. "The Next Step in World Politics: A United States of Europe." Scottish Opinion 2 (Nov. 1947): 11.

Power foresees a United States of Europe with Scotland taking a leading role in the championing of smaller nations.

236. Ramsay, M.P. "The Scotland I'd Like to See." New Scot 2 (March 1947): 24-27.

Ramsay draws parallels between a free Scotland and the ideal of the ancient Greek city-state.

237.   Smith, A. Clark. "The Future of Nationalism." Scots
Socialist (1947): 3.

   Challenges Labour's war policy in Scotland. Questions the
   storage of nuclear weapons on Scottish soil.

238.   Thaw, Robert. "The Facade and the Bield." New Alliance
1 (June/July 1940): 3-5.

   World War II has drawn the facade, Thaw writes, revealing
   English totalitarianism. Scotland should strike for
   independence immediately or risk being drawn into war for
   England's sake.

239.   Urquhart, James. "Afterthoughts on the Home Rule
Assembly." New Scot 3 (May 1947): 20-22.

   Comments on a multi-party conference on Scottish Home
   Rule held on March 22, 1947, representing all shades of
   opinion on Home Rule. Urquhart concludes that the Labour
   Party is the true party of Home Rule.

240.   Urquhart, James. "Scottish Home Rule: the Labour View."
Forum 1 (Aug./Sept. 1947): 9-10.

   A defense of the Labour Party's position on Scottish Home
   Rule, its historical support for Home Rule, and the
   likelihood of a Labour Government achieving that for
   Scotland.

241.   Walkinshaw, Colin. "A Government for Scotland." Scots
Review 11 (May 1950): 23.

   Investigates the type of government Scottish tradition
   would indicate - an orthodox democracy with a president
   and cabinet, with strong democracy at the local level.
   (Walkinshaw is a pseudonym for James Reid.)

242.   Walkinshaw, Colin. "A Government for Scotland - 2."
Scots Review 11 (June 1950): 46.

   A warning against the dangers of vested interests and
   the threat they pose to representative government.

243.   Walkinshaw, Colin. "A Government for Scotland - 3."
Scots Review 11 (July 1950): 64.

   Walkinshaw foresees a Parliament of two houses, with
   devolution of powers to local government, plus a special
   senate given over to interest groups.

244. Walkinshaw, Colin. "In Unity to Dwell." New Alliance 6 (Jan./Feb 1945): 1-3.

Unity can be a mask for totalitarianism, thus, a highly individualistic Scotland should not opt for a false unity in government, this writer warns.

245. Walkinshaw, Colin. "Lesson from a Ghost." New Alliance 6 (Dec./Jan. 1946): 1-2.

States lessons to be learned from Ireland's independence. Scotland, like Ireland, should make the most of existing institutions in order to secure Home Rule.

246. Walkinshaw, Colin. "The New Covenanters." Scots Review 10 (Dec. 1949): 159.

How the Covenant is proof of the depth of Scottish demand for self-rule and evidence of its sincerity.

247. Walkinshaw, Colin. "Prospect for Scotland." New Alliance 2 (Dec./Jan. 1941): 3-4.

Walkinshaw claims that an English victory in World War II will increase her arrogance and make Scottish Home Rule even more difficult. Scotland should begin to control her own resources, even during the War.

248. Walkinshaw, Colin."Prospect for Scotland - II." New Alliance 2 (Feb./March 1941): 3-4.

Furthers the argument that only a self-governing Scotland can meet the needs of a chaotic post-war Europe.

249. Walkinshaw, Colin. "Prospect for Scotland - III." New Alliance 2 (April/May 1941): 3-5.

In planning for a new government, Scotland should enact agrarian reform immediately.

250. Walkinshaw, Colin. "Prospect for Scotland - IV." New Alliance 2 (June/July 1941): 4-6.

The writer asks what type of government would best suit an independent Scotland. He makes the claim for a parliamentary democracy having a governor, president, or regent.

251. Walkinshaw, Colin. "What's Wrong with Fascism?" New Alliance 3 (Oct./Nov. 1942): 1-3.

Those fearing fascism in Scotland should remember that Scotland's long tradition of democracy and freedom will render that unlikely, despite its success elsewhere, writes Walkinshaw.

252. Wilson, John. "Scottish Home Rule - The Liberal View."
Forum 1 (Dec. 1946): 9-10.

A history of the support the Liberal Party has given to
Home Rule; its notion of Scottish participation in a
Federal British State and its concept of divided powers
into purely Scottish affairs vs. affairs of the United
Kingdom as a whole, including defense and foreign policy.
This federal idea has a long and respected tradition in
Scottish Nationalism.

253. Wood, Wendy. "The Auld Alliance." National Weekly 4
(April 26, 1952): 2-3.

Compares Scotland's position today with her position in
the 14th century. Alliance with Ireland against England
could thus parallel the "Auld Alliance" between France
and Scotland in the 14th century.

254. Wood, Wendy. "Taking of the Stone of Destiny: Reactions
Favorable and Otherwise." National Weekly 2 (Feb. 3, 1951): 2.

A summary of the favorable comments Wendy Wood received
from both sides of the border, defending the taking of
the Stone of Scone by Scottish Nationalists in December
1950.

255. Wood, Wendy. "What is Freedom Worth?" National Weekly 3
(April 14, 1951): 3.

In Ireland for Easter celebrations, Wood asks the price
of freedom, considering the great improvement in Irish
life, and questions the value of young Scots dying in
Korea while conditions are yet so bad in Scotland.

256. Wood, Wendy. "What Next?" National Weekly 4 (March 1,
1952): 2.

Wood advocates international recognition of Scotland's
claim to nationhood. She urges a meeting of the Three
Estates (Nobility, Church, and Burghs) in a
Scottish Parliament to declare a General Election for
Scotland only, with preparations to defend against
English armed interference.

257. Young, Douglas. "The Re-Colonisation of Scotland."
Scots Review 7 (April 1946): 2.

Young finds agrarian reform as the great task of a
free Scotland. He outlines here the complexities of
the land problem and archaic land laws.

258. Young, Douglas. "Scottish Land and Living." Lion Rampant 1 (1947): 5-7.

Young's ideas on a land policy for an independent Scotland. He uses the owner-worker system in Denmark as a model rather than the collective system used in the Ukraine.

259. Young, Douglas. "Scottish Nationalism and the Federal Union." Scots Independent (January 1940): 9.

Young urges Scots to resist conscription in order to show how undemocratic England really is. Young and others in Scotland went to prison for their anti-war activities.

260. Young, Douglas. "The Survival of Scotland." Scots Review 11 (February 1951): 199.

Young asks how Scottish nationality has managed to survive over the centuries against such great odds. He answers with examples from church, clan, regiment, local and regional customs, music, dance, sport, and others. He finds several characteristics which might guarantee Scottish nationality.

261. Young, Douglas. "To Freeminded Scots." Scots Independent (April 1943): 5.

While serving a 12 month sentence for conscientious objection to World War II, Young compares Scotland to the world within Saughton Prison. He concludes that both worlds are worlds devoid of choice and freedom.

262. Young, Douglas. "Why I Signed the Covenant." National Weekly 2 (Nov. 26, 1949): 5.

Young's reply to Hugh MacDiarmid, who refused to sign the Covenant. MacDiarmid criticized the Covenant for being too conservative and cautious in its approach to Scottish freedom. However, Young states here that he signed it because it was an excellent chance for most Scots to have their true opinions recorded.

4.

1960–1974: THE ROCKY ROAD TO WESTMINSTER

The landscape should belong to the people who see it all the time.

LeRoi Jones, (Amiri Baraka)
1966

Struggles for recognition in the early decades of the twentieth century bore political fruit in the sixties. Nationalists claimed steady support in the polls, with Winifred Ewing winning the by-election in Hamilton in 1967, the first nationalist electoral victory in 22 years. Hopes for economic prosperity sparked by North Sea oil brought unprecedented success, culminating in the October, 1974, General Election, when Scottish Nationalists captured 30.4% of the vote. For the first time in history, Scottish Nationalists could force compromise from the major parties. With this new respect and influence in Westminster, Scottish and Welsh Nationalists could take a next step: create legislation that would produce independence or devolution. Almost immediately, bills giving some measure of self-government were envisioned. With great optimism, the stage for independence was set. As MacDiarmid and others put it: "the heather was on fire."

BOOKS AND PAMPHLETS

263. Alexander, K.J.W. "The Economic Case Against
Independence." In The Scottish Debate, edited by Neil
MacCormick, 132-142. Oxford: Oxford U. Press, 1970.

Using charts and tables to prove his case, the author
concludes that independence, economically, would be a
"desolating experience" for Scotland.

264. Banks, J.C. Federal Britain? London: Harrap, 1971.
336pp. bibl.

Banks presents the case for regional devolution in the
United Kingdom, and pays particular attention to
Scotland and Wales. He explores what he terms the "myth"
of British unity. "Confraternity" is seen as one solution
to the problem of centralization and London-based power.
European regions may also be an answer. Banks sees
devolution as a move to true democracy in Britain and
in Europe.

265. Bell, R.E. "Home Rule and the Scottish Universities."
In Government and Nationalism in Scotland, edited by
J.N. Wolfe, 108-119. Edinburgh: Edinburgh University Press,
1969.

Investigates the present financial and admission policies
of the Scottish Universities. Bell studies the complaint
that Scottish students are discriminated against by
English funding procedures. He suggests that a special
committee should be set up to study the claims.

266. Blalock, Hubert M. Jr. Toward a Theory of Minority
Group Relations. London: John Wiley, 1967. 227pp.

A comprehensive and technical study of all factors
affecting race relations and the treatment of minorities.
The class and size of minority groups are studied in
great detail. Based on studies of black-white relations
in the U.S.A. many conclusions and methods would also
apply to minorities in Britain, including the Scots
and Welsh.

267. Brand, Jack, and Cornford, J.P. "Scottish Voting
Behaviour." In Government and Nationalism in Scotland, edited
by J.N. Wolfe, 17-40. Edinburgh: Edinburgh University Press,
1969.

A study of British voting patterns, with special
emphasis on those who supported the Scottish National
Party. The authors conclude that voters who voted for
the Scottish National Party came from a wide range of
backgrounds and classes.

268. Brown, Oliver. Witdom. Glasgow: Maclellan, 1969. 134 pp.

Forward by Hugh MacDiarmid. A humorous collection of
anecdotes and aphorisms by an editor, socialist, and
nationalist. Brown talks of "The Menace of Hugeness"
and of "The Influence of the English in Scotland."
Typical Brown: "The Lord in his wisdom gave us the
Cheviots as a defensive barrier. We really needed the
Alps."

269. Buchanan, Keith. "Economic Growth and Cultural
Liquidation: the Case of the Celtic Nations." In The Celtic
League Annual, 7-27. Dublin: The Celtic League, 1970.

Economic progress in the Celtic nations has often meant
culture and language decline, yet Buchanan finds even
this progress temporary and superficial. He calls for
nationalist parties to protect culture while making sure
that money is invested in projects that have lasting
benefit to the people most affected by them.

270. Buchanan, Keith, and Armstrong, Warwick. "The Roots of
Scottish and Welsh Nationalism." In The Celtic League Annual,
12-30. Dublin: The Celtic League, 1968.

The writers conclude that the collapse of the British
Empire has left Wales and Scotland to fend for themselves.
The only answer to former colonialism and exploitation
is to form strong nationalist parties that resort neither
to colonialism nor to exploitation.

271. Buchanan, Keith, and Armstrong, Warwick. "Welsh and
Scottish Nationalism: 20th Century." In The Celtic League
Annual, 7-21. Dublin: The Celtic League, 1969.

The authors touch on the links between economic and
cultural exploitation. Cultural death brings defeatism
which in turn brings passivity, they argue, therefore,
"intellectual colonization" must end before any true
economic progress can be made.

272. The Celtic League. Celtic Advance in the Atomic Age:
Annual Volume of the Celtic League. Dublin: The Celtic
League, 1967. 123pp.

Chapters specifically on Scotland: "Political Advance
in Scotland," and "Scotland and Gaelic." Also deals
with bilingualism in all the Celtic nations of Europe.

273. The Celtic League. Maintaining a National Identity:
The Celtic League Annual. Dublin: The Celtic League, 1968.
167pp.

Includes: "The Roots of Scottish and Welsh Nationalism"
and "Celtic Scotland on the Fringe of Europe."

274. Donaldson, Gordon. "Scottish Devolution: the Historical
Backgound." In Government and Nationalism in Scotland,
edited by J.N. Wolfe, 4-16. Edinburgh: Edinburgh University
Press, 1969.

     Donaldson posits three key phases in Scotland's Union
     with England. To 1750, general discontent; to 1850,
     general acceptance; to the present, general criticism
     but based on the fortunes of the Union as a whole.

275. Edwards, Owen D.; Evans, Gwynfor; and MacDiarmid, Hugh.
Celtic Nationalism. London: Routledge, 1968. 358pp.

     Sections on Ireland, Wales, and Scotland. MacDiarmid
     argues that Scots are mismanaged and exploited by
     Westminster. He lists special Scottish needs in education,
     industry, tourism, employment, etc. He discusses the
     Scottish National Party at great length. For each topic,
     he considers the benefits independence would bring for
     Scotland.

276. Ellis, P. Beresford. The Creed of the Celtic Revolution.
London: Medusa Press, 1969. 32pp.

     Ellis proposes a union of the Celtic nations of Europe
     as a solution to their cultural and economic decline.
     Ellis is especially interested in language revival
     in the Celtic nations. A Union of Brittany, Ireland,
     Wales, Scotland, Man, and Cornwall would provide a
     united front against exploitation.

277. Erickson, John. "Scotland's Defence Commitment: Some
Problems of Cost, Capability and Effectiveness." In
Government and Nationalism in Scotland, 71-87. Edinburgh:
Edinburgh University Press, 1969.

     A model for defence spending in an independent or
     devolved Scotland.

278. Evans, Gwynfor. "Freedom for All Nations." In Book
of the Celtic League, 7-10. Dublin, The Celtic League, 1965.

     Evans argues that socialism must resist the cultural
     destruction of imperialism by supporting independence
     for smaller nations and regions.

279. Evans, Gwynfor. "Scotland's Case." In Book of the
Celtic League, 60-70. Dublin: The Celtic League, 1965.

     Evans finds no legal case for continuance of Union, and
     points to Scotland's separate church, legal system,
     and education as proof of Scottish nationhood.

280. Ewing, Winifred. "Nationalism is Progress." In Celtic League Annual, 9-11. Dublin: The Celtic League, 1968.

Ewing writes of replacing the "False unity of dominion" with the "true unity of co-operative enterprise", to the democratic benefit of both Scotland and England.

281. Feirabend, I.K.,ed. Anger, Violence and Politics: Theories and Research. Englewood Cliffs, New Jersey, 1972. 423pp.

Theories of revolution and studies and case histories of political violence. Investigates why some movements have erupted in violence while others have not. The chapter on Scotland is entitled: "The Scottish National Party: Nonviolent Separatism and Theories of Violence." The SNP is studied as a model of a fairly successful but non-violent political group.

282. Fowler, John, ed. Bannerman: The Memoirs of Lord Bannerman of Kildonan. Aberdeen: Impulse Books, 1972. 133pp.

Biography of Bannerman and his involvement with the Gaelic League, the Liberal Party, and his activities on behalf of the Gaelic language and of Home Rule. Bannerman died in 1969.

283. Glen, Duncan. "Nation or Region?" In Whither Scotland? edited by Duncan Glen, 9-23. London: Gollancz, 1971.

Glen provides a general background to Scotland's cultural and political malaise. He sees the issue as one of culture and psychology as much as one of politics. His vision: "a Scottish Scotland with a European outlook."

284. Glen, Duncan, ed. Whither Scotland? A Prejudiced Look at the Future of a Nation. London: Gollancz, 1971. 255pp.

Collection of essays by various authors: "Nation or Region?", "Education","Gaelic Scotland", "The Future of Scots", "Politics", and many more, all touching on nationalism or nationhood to some degree.

285. Greenberg, William. The Flags of the Forgotten. Brighton: Clifton, 1969. 158pp.

An objective account of the nationalism of Scotland, Wales, Man, and Cornwall. Strengths and weaknesses of the movements of each. Greenberg concludes that modern nationalism in Britain is not a temporary phenomenon, but must be taken seriously.

286. Hanham, Harry J. Scottish Nationalism. London: Faber,
1969. 250pp. bibl.

Hanham, a native of New Zealand, has taught in several
countries and brings this diverse national experience
to bear on many themes: "The Scottishness of Scottish
Society", "The Rise and Fall of Literary Nationalism,"
and many more. This is one of the key works of the
decade on Scottish Nationalism. The work was praised by
MacDiarmid and others for its objective treatment of
modern nationalism and of the Scottish National Party.

287. Kedourie, Elie. Nationalism. London: Hutchinson, 1966.
151pp.

This work is mentioned in most bibliographies as a very
influential work. It is frequently alluded to by
Scottish Nationalists. Kedourie touches on many crucial
themes, including nationalism and socialism, self-
determination, and the state and the individual.

288. Kellas, James. Modern Scotland: the Nation Since 1870.
London: Pall Mall, 1968. 284pp.

Religion, law, education, government, economics, etc.
Kellas finds a strong sense of nationhood and Scottish-
ness on the increase due to the troubles confronting
Britain as a whole. The coverage of this work includes
the several nationalist movements in Scotland since
Home Rule in the 1880's.

289. Kennedy, Gavin. "Scotland's Economy." In The Radical
Approach: Papers on an Independent Scotland, edited by
Gavin Kennedy, 47-59. Edinburgh: Palingenesis Press, 1976.

Kennedy studies the domination of the Scottish economy
by powerful English and American multinationals.
Kennedy notes that exploitation of the Third World
by these companies is deplored while nothing is done
to prevent the same treatment in Scotland. An
independent Scotland could not allow this to happen.

290. Kloss, Heinz. "Problems of Nationality in Europe Today."
In Book of the Celtic League, edited by Ceirwen Thomas, 62-
70. Cardiff: The Celtic League, 1963.

A call for the "have" nations of Europe to assist states
which have to struggle to maintain their culture and
nationhood.

291. Kohn, Hans. Nationalism: its Meaning and History.
NY: Van Nostrand, 1965. 191pp.

A concise history of nationalism, illustrated by writings
by Herder, Hegel, Nehru, Mao, Mussolini, Douglas Hyde and
others. A standard work on nationalism.

292. Linklater, Eric. The Survival of Scotland: A Review
of Scottish History from Roman Times to the Present Day.
London: Heinemann, 1968. 376pp.

> Devoted mainly to history up to the nineteenth century,
> but Linklater's theme of Scottish survival has relevance
> to Scottish Nationalism.

293. MacCormick, Iain S.M. "The Case for Independence."
In The Scottish Debate, edited by Neil MacCormick, 89-102.
Oxford: Oxford U. Press, 1970.

> Historical sketch of Scotland's desire for self-rule
> Inequality within Britain makes the British Union
> undesirable, states MacCormick, and the idea of Union
> should thus have ended with the end of the Empire which
> sustained that idea.

294. MacCormick, Neil. "Independence and Constitutional
Change." In The Scottish Debate, edited by Neil MacCormick,
52-64. Oxford: Oxford U. Press, 1970.

> MacCormick examines the constitutional options open to
> an independent Scotland and discusses in turn, devolution,
> federation, and complete independence.

295. MacCormick, Neil. The Scottish Debate: Essays on
Scottish Nationalism. Oxford: Oxford U. Press, 1970. 160pp.

> Collection of essays (pro and con) on various aspects
> of Scottish Nationalism. History, law, defence, economics,
> federalism, etc. Objective and provocative.

296. Mackenzie, Compton. My Life and Times, Octave Seven
1931-1938. London: Chatto and Windus, 1968. 320pp.

> Autobiography. Covers the years of Mackenzie's
> involvement with nationalism in Scotland. Reports on
> his famous victory in the Glasgow University Rectorial
> Election, in October, 1931. This volume includes his
> famous rectorial address given on January 29, 1932.

297. Mackintosh, John P. The Devolution of Power: Local
Democracy, Regionalism and Nationaism. London: Chatto and
Windus, 1968. 207pp.

> Mackintosh proposes solutions to the problems of
> democracy in centralized Britain. See: Chapter 7,
> "Welsh and Scottish Nationalism," Chapter 8, "Meeting
> the Nationalist Case," and finally, "Conclusion: a
> Workable Regionalism for England, Scotland, and
> Wales." Mackintosh believes the solution is to be found
> in elected regional councils, with those in Wales and
> Scotland having a large measure of autonomy.

298. McLaren, Moray. If Freedom Fail. London: Secker and
Warburg, 1964. 350pp.

McLaren traces the idea of Scots freedom and rebellion
through Bannockburn, Flodden, the Union of 1707, and
beyond. He believes the majority of Scots want self-
government and sees federalism as one option among
many.

299. McLaughlan, Robert. "Aspects of Nationalism." In
The Scottish Debate, edited by Neil MacCormick, 21-33.
Oxford: Oxford U. Press, 1970.

A strong polemic against the notion of an independent
Scotland. Independence would ignore the fundamental
divisions of class, religion, and economics that exist
in Scotland, McLaughlan observes. He also argues that
Scottish Nationalism could possibly lead to a tyranny
of the right or left. He favors democratic reforms
rather than drastic change.

300. Marwick, William H. James Barr: Modern Covenanter.
Penicuik: Scots Secretariat, 1973. 16pp.

Outline of Barr's life-his membership in the Scottish
Home Rule Association and Independent Labour Party, and
his pacifism in World War II. Short bibliography of
Barr's works included.

301. Miller, Karl., ed. Memoirs of a Modern Scotland.
London: Faber and Faber, 1970. 206pp.

A collection of essays on Scottish culture by various
contributors. See especially, "Scottish Nationalism
since 1918," by Arthur Marwick, and the widely
discussed "The Three Dreams of Scottish Nationalism" by
Tom Nairn.

302. Murchison, T.M. "The Nationalist Movement in Scotland."
In Celtic League Annual, 28-35. Dublin: The Celtic League,
1969.

An excellent general sketch of Scottish independence
movements from 1707, through the Home Rule demands of
the late 19th century up to April, 1969.

303. Murison, D.D. "Nationalism as Expressed in Scottish
Literature." In Government and Nationalism in Scotland,
edited by J.N. Wolfe, 189-199. Edinburgh: Edinburgh University
Press, 1969.

Scottish literary nationalism from Barbour's Brus,
to Sir Walter Scott, to moderns like C.M. Grieve and
Lewis Grassic Gibbon.

304. Murray, David. "The Dynamic of Self Government." In
The Celtic League Annual, 25-28. Dublin: The Celtic League,
1967.

  The present differences between Scotland and England
  are seen as part of a historical dynamic: Liberal vs.
  Tory, Labour vs. Liberal, Socialism vs. Capitalism,
  and now, he believes, Regionalism vs. Centralism.

305. Murray, David. The First Nation in Europe: a Portrait
of Scotland and the Scots. London: Pall Mall Press, 1960.
143pp.

  Murray "seeks formative causes of the Scottishness of
  Scotland." Examines Scottish law, education, church,
  art and literature, industry, politics, and emigration.

306. Murray, Duncan C. "Celtic Scotland on the Fringe of
Europe." In Celtic League Annual, 95-100. Dublin: The Celtic
League, 1968.

  Dismisses idea of "fringe" Scotland. Murray notes how
  scholars and saints from this so-called fringe once
  revived the culture of Europe, and can do so again
  if political independence is achieved.

307. Neil, William. "Is Scotland a Celtic Nation?" In
The Celtic League Annual, edited by Frank Thomson, 73-77.
Dublin: The Celtic League, 1970.

  Neil concludes that Scotland is primarily Celtic but
  must do more to understand its Celtic heritage.
  Political independence would encourage that understanding
  Neil states.

308. Paton, Herbert J. The Claim of Scotland. London: Allen
and Unwin, 1968. 279pp.

  Paton builds up an objective and factual case for
  Scottish independence by considering taxation, employment,
  bureaucracy, and the benefits that would result to
  England from Scottish self-rule. He considers all of the
  possible objections to Scottish independence and trys to
  answer them in great detail. He chronicles most of the
  arguments for and against Scottish Home Rule. This book
  has been praised for its careful objectivity and
  disinterest. MacDiarmid considered that English refusal
  to listen to such a book was final proof that only
  militant action by Scotland would achieve independence.

309. Phillipson, N.T. "Nationalism and Ideology." In
Government and Nationalism in Scotland, edited by J.N.Wolfe,
167-188. Edinburgh: Edinburgh U. Press, 1969.

  Historical sketch of Scottish middle class attitudes to
  Scottish Nationalism.

310.   Scwarz, John E. "The Scottish National Party: Nonviolent Separatism and Theories of Violence." In Anger, Violence and Politics: Theories and Research, edited by I.K. Feirabend, 325-341. Englewood Cliffs, New Jersey: Prentice Hall, 1972.

Schwarz investigates the Scottish National Party to learn how a separatist movement can remain essentially nonviolent while maintaining a strong political position. He views the Scottish National Party as a model for theorists studying the nature of violence and nonviolence in modern politics.

311.   The Scots Secretariat. Scotland's Scrap of Paper. Penicuik: The Scots Secretariat, 1971. 64pp.

Includes a full text of the Treaty of Union of 1707. On pages 52-54 is a brief history of self-government proposals put before Parliament from 1889-1927. Also included is a section on the "Policy of the National Party of Scotland, 1928-1934."

312.   Simpson, David. "Independence: the Economic Issues." In The Scottish Debate, edited by Neil MacCormick, 121-131. Oxford: Oxford U. Press, 1970.

Simpson contends that an independent Scotland would be a richer Scotland in the long run, while acknowledging that statistics are difficult to evaluate to prove this. He also believes that Scottish dependence has been deliberately encouraged by foreign investors and by the British Establishment.

313.   Smith, T.B. "Scottish Nationalism, Law and Self-Government." In The Scottish Debate, edited by Neil MacCormick, 34-51. Oxford: Oxford U. Press, 1970.

A full explanation of the unique features of the current Scottish legal system and how the system might function in an independent Scotland.

314.   Steel, David. "Federalism." In The Scottish Debate, edited by Neil MacCormick, 80-88. Oxford: Oxford U. Press, 1970.

Steel, the leader of the Liberal Party, defends the Liberal Party policy of federalism for Scotland. He contrasts federalism with regionalism and separatism. He views successful instances of federalism in the USA, Canada, Yugoslavia, and Switzerland. A thorough discussion of the federal concept. Federalism has been the official position of the Liberal Party on Scotland and Wales throughout the century.

315. Stevenson, David. "Political Advance in Scotland."
In Celtic League Annual, 43-46. Dublin: The Celtic League,
1967.

A summary of the views of the Scottish National Party up
to 1967.

316. Thayer, George. The British Political Fringe: a Profile.
London: Blond, 1965. 256pp.

An investigation of diverse parties and groups outside
the mainstream of British politics, including the
Campaign for Nuclear Disarmament, the Welsh, Cornish,
Irish, and Scottish national parties, and various groups
from the far left and far right. Chapter 10 is entitled
"The Scottish Nationalists". It deals with the several
groups working for Scottish independence in the mid-
sixties.

317. Thomas, Ceirwen, ed., The Celtic Nations: the Book of
the Celtic League. Cardiff: The Celtic League, 1963. 79pp.

On Scotland: "The Voice of Scotland", "Scotland Now",
and "The Problems of Nationality in Europe Today".

318. Thompson, Frank, ed., The Celt in the Seventies: The
Celtic League Annual. Dublin: The Celtic League, 1970. 192pp.

A summary of the language, culture, politics, and future
of the Celtic nations, including Scotland.

319. Thompson, Frank, ed., The Significance of Freedom:
The Celtic League Annual. Dublin: The Celtic League, 1969.
155pp.

"Welsh and Scottish Nationalism", and "The Nationalist
Movement in Scotland".

320. Thompson, F.G. "Scotland Now." In Book of the Celtic
League, edited by Ceirwen Thomas, 45-49. Cardiff: The
Celtic League, 1963.

Unemployment and emigration have resulted in an increase
in support for Scottish Nationalism, observes Thompson,
and he expects this support to continue and increase as
Britain's problems worsen.

321. Thompson, Frank. "The Voice of Scotland." in Book of
the Celtic League, edited by Ceirwen Thomas, 40-44. Cardiff:
The Celtic League, 1963.

On the significance of "pirate radio" in promoting Welsh
and Scottish independence.

322. Thompson, George., ed. Recent Developments in the
Celtic League: Annual Book of the Celtic League. Dublin:
The Celtic League, 1966. 101pp.

     See especially, "New Hope for Gaelic," and "Scotland
     Today."

323. Thornhill, W. The Case for Regional Reform. London:
Nelson, 1972. 269pp.

     Various official documents are presented surveying
     the many proposals for regional government in Britain.
     Pages 39-43 deal with Scottish Nationalism from 1920
     onwards and its challenge to central government.
     Nationalism is seen by Thornhill as simply a demand
     for true democracy.

324. Wolfe, Billy. Scotland Lives. Edinburgh: Reprographia,
1973. 167pp.

     A political autobiography dealing with Wolfe's
     practical involvement in local politics and his
     leadership of the Scottish National Party. Wolfe details
     the events of the important 1962 West Lothian by-election
     which helped establish the SNP as an important force
     in Scottish politics once again.

325. Wolfe, J.N. Government and Nationalism in Scotland:
an Enquiry by Members of the University of Edinburgh.
Edinburgh: Edinburgh University Press, 1969. 205pp.

     Based on the Fifth Edinburgh Seminar in the Social
     Sciences, held Dec.7-8, 1968. Its theme was "Nationalism
     and Scotland." Some topics: Home Rule and the university,
     nationalism in Scottish literature, the financial
     problems of independence, etc. An important work of the
     decade.

326. Wood, Wendy. Yours Sincerely for Scotland: the Autobiography of a Patriot. London: Arthur Barker, 1970. 262pp.

     Autobiography from early days in South Africa to
     involvement in Scottish Nationalism from 1916.
     Chapter 3, "Nationalism" is especially pertinent.

327. Wright, Esmond. "In Defence of the United Kingdom."
In The Scottish Debate, edited by Neil MacCormick, 103-120.
Oxford: Oxford U. Press, 1970.

     Wright believes that the United Kingdom needs revision,
     improvement, and greater democracy, but denies that
     Scottish independence would provide any of these things.
     He views the United Kingdom as a historical necessity,
     with Scotland as a vital ingredient.

328. Wright, L.C. "Some Fiscal Problems of Devolution in
Scotland." In Government and Nationalsim in Scotland, edited
by J.N. Wolfe, 140-152. Edinburgh: Edinburgh U. Press, 1969.

   This article studies the problems of wealth distribution
   in a future self-governing Scotland.

329. Young, Douglas. "A Sketch History of Scottish Nationalism." In The Scottish Debate, edited by Neil MacCormick, 5-
20. Oxford: Oxford U. Press, 1970.

   Young provides a general but complete overview of
   Scottish nationality from the earliest times to the
   present. Short, but informative.

330. Young, Douglas. Scotland. London: Cassell, 1971. 268pp.

   Douglas Young, poet, nationalist, classical scholar,
   writes a book on all aspects of Scottish culture and
   government. "Politics and Power Groups" and "Languages,
   Literatures and the Mass Media" are particularly
   relevant to Scottish Nationalism. Factual and entertain-
   ing.

ARTICLES

331. Baur, Chris. "Scottish Government: a Kind of Consensus."
Scottish International 5 (March 1972): 7.

   On Feb. 14, 1972, a Scottish Trade Union Conference on
   unemployment revealed vast sentiment for political
   freedom in Scotland. Baur finds this support likely
   to increase as Scotland's economy worsens.

332. Boothby, F.A.C. "Looking In: the Border." Catalyst
(Spring 1969):5.

   Boothby thinks the border with England should pose no
   problem when independence comes, citing the French-
   Spanish border and the USA-Canadian border as
   successful, peaceful boundaries.

333. Boothby, F.A.C. "Looking In: U.D.I?" Catalyst
(Autumn 1968): 5-6.

   Boothby discusses the practicality of "Unilateral
   Declaration of Independence" in Scotland, a procedure
   that worked for Rhodesia. Instead of UDI, he urges a
   legal case for "instant recognition" by a foreign
   power as a means to gather international acceptance
   of an independent, legal, and progressive Scotland.

334. Boothby, F.A.C. "On Federalism." Catalyst (Autumn 1969):
14.

Federalism has not worked in the USA, Canada, Malaysia,
Nigeria, etc. argues Boothby, so why should it work
in Great Britain? Federalism has many adherents in
Scotland, but here's an article that challenges its
desirability.

335. Boothby, F.A.C. "A Proposal for a Confederate League."
Sgian Dubh 6(September 1969): 6.

Boothby makes the distinction between limited federation
and sovereign confederation and believes all of the
Celtic nations should opt for confederation.

336. Brown, Oliver. "This Golden Age of Personality."
Catalyst (Winter 1968): 15-16.

A catalog of key Scottish Nationalists: Lewis Spence,
MacDiarmid, Muirhead, MacCormick, William Power and
others.

337. Cleary, O.A. "The Self-Government Dilemma." Catalyst
(Autumn 1969): 28-30.

Comment on the gap between nationalists who desire
Scottish independence and the masses who don't .
Cleary believes the SNP must work harder to persuade
Scots of the benefits of self-rule.

338. Dicken, John. "Whither Scotland?" Catalyst (Spring 1968)
12-13.

The convenor of the SNP Foreign Affairs Committee
envisions a non-aligned, non-partisan, independent
Scotland, free of NATO, and having close Third World
ties.

339. Hall, John G. "A Short History of the Scottish National
Movement." Catalyst (Spring 1968): 22-23.

From the 1886 Scottish Home Rule Association to the
election victory of 1967.

340. Hargrave, Andrew. "The Economics of Devolution."
Scottish International (Oct./Nov. 1968): 10-17.

Hargrave considers economic realities and theories, and
cautions against comparing Scotland with other small
nations. He believes Scotland can afford independence,
but can also benefit from having close economic ties to
England and Wales.

341. Hargrave, Andrew. "Politics of Devolution." Scottish International (Jan. 1969): 9-11.

Hargrave lists some problems and solutions of devolution of finance, administration, Parliament, and local government.

342. Harvie, Christopher. "The Democrat Game." Scottish International (Sept. 1969): 3-5.

Harvie challenges the assumption that presupposes democracy in an independent Scotland. He points out that despite Scotland's historical reputation for freedom, the influence of Calvinism and its reliance on authority is also very strong.

343. Herdman, John. "Using the Enemy's Weapons." Catalyst (Spring 1969): 5.

Article states how cultural nationalism is often more potent and revolutionary than mere political nationalism.

344. Heusaff, Alan. "The Celtic League." Catalyst (Summer 1969): 20-23.

Heusaff explains the aims and history of the League, founded in Wales in 1961, to promote ties between Brittany, Cornwall, Wales, the Isle of Man, Scotland, and Ireland.

345. Hughson, Irene I. "The Celtic Fringe-Couldn't We Change its Name?" Catalyst (Spring 1970): 25-26.

Hughson objects to "Celtic" as a hazy and inaccurate term, not suited to the exigencies of twentieth century politics. She concludes that a truly dynamic Scottish or Welsh Nationalism would have no use for the term.

346. Legonna, John. "Celtic Union-Dreamer's Mumble or Next Step?" Catalyst (Winter 1970): 25-27.

Proposes a Celtic "hub" rather than "fringe" e.g. one Celtic nation with one capital, one administration, and six key regions.

347. MacDonald, Ian. "Nationalism: the Third Renaissance." Catalyst (Summer 1969): 8.

Scottish Nationalism is seen by MacDonald as a reflection of a worldwide seeking of personal and national liberation. Scotland's quest is thus one that should receive much understanding and support throughout the world.

348. MacInnes, Colin. "Scotland: a nation reviving." New Society (July 11, 1974): 71-73.

North Sea oil and growing Scottish Nationalism.

349. McKendrick, Hamish. "Secession." Catalyst (December 1967): 4-5.

An argument for immediate and unconditional secession by Scotland from Great Britain.

350. McKendrick, Hamish. "Seven Steps to Freedom." Catalyst (Spring 1968): 20-21.

McKendrick's seven steps: elect 36 nationalist M.P.'s; maneuver in Parliament; issue an ultimatum for independence, which would probably go unheeded, so form a Scottish Parliament; proclaim independence; form a cabinet; gain international recognition; be prepared to back claim up with force.

351. McLaren, Moray. "English Nationalism." Catalyst (December 1967): 12-13.

Scottish Nationalism, notes McLaren, would result in a truer English Nationalism, which would benefit England enormously. He believes the net result would be more democracy throughout the British Isles.

352. MacWilliam, Ian. "Down with Nationalism." Catalyst (Spring 1970): 24.

MacWilliam thinks "nationalism" is a bad term with unpleasant connotations. He believes Scots should do away with the term and concentrate on achieving independence.

353. MacWilliam, Ian. "George Orwell on Scottish Nationalism" Catalyst (Summer 1970): 23-24.

Explains Orwell's normal hostility to Scotland and to nationalism in general and how this attitude softened while he was resident on Jura in the 1940's and seeing the problem of landlordism first-hand.

354. Maxwell, Stephen. "Treason of the Clerks." Scottish International 5 (August, 1972): 18-20.

Maxwell analyzes the cultural and political importance of the high ratio of English professors, lecturers, and students in Scottish universities.

355. Moffat, George. "The Marketing of a Political Ideal."
Catalyst (Winter 1968): 3-4.

   Moffat thinks that Scottish Nationalists have a poor
   public image and should use proper marketing and
   advertising techniques to reach the public.

356. Morrison, David. "Meat for Argument." Catalyst (Spring
1970): 28-29.

   A criticism of Orwell's essay "Notes on Nationalism"
   which first appeared in 1945. Morrison doesn't think
   that Scottish Nationalism is based on greed and self-
   deception, two ingredients Orwell believed defined
   all forms of nationalism.

357. Murphy, John. "Roland E. Muirhead." Catalyst (Spring
1969): 15-16.

   Traces the life of Muirhead from Lochwinnoch, stressing
   his enormous contributions to Scottish Nationalism.
   Muirhead died in 1964.

358. Rankin, William. "Scotland First?" New Society (April
18, 1974): 128-130.

   Rankin traces 100 years of Scottish Nationalist in-
   fighting, disagreement, and political merger and survival.

359. Scott, Tom. "Ends Before Means." Scotia Review (Dec.
1972): 3-5.

   Nationalization of land, a constitution and bill of
   rights, and a freely elected government should be
   Scotland's priorities states Scott.

360. The Scottish National Party. "Memorandum from the SNP."
Catalyst (Summer 1968): 19-20.

   A memorandum delivered to 27 European states stating
   the desire of Scotland's friendship in return for a
   respect for Scotland's right to sovereignty.

361. Sinner, William K. "The Warp and the Woof." Catalyst
(Autumn 1968): 30-31.

   A synopsis of Scottish radical movements from 1745 to
   the present.

362. Taylor, Ian. "Genesis and Exodus." Catalyst (Spring
1968): 8-9.

   Explains the name and purpose of the 1320 Club and the
   famous Declaration of Arbroath in 1320. Taylor believes
   in Scotland's right of secession and also believes she
   should first seek international recognition.

363. Wolfe, William. "SNP and the Arts." <u>Scottish International</u> 1 (April 1968): 5-6.

What a self-governing Scotland could do for the nation's arts.

364. Wood, Wendy. "Independence is not Enough." <u>Catalyst</u> (Summer 1969): 15.

Wood argues that Scottish independence must be cultural as well as political.

5.

1975–1979: SCOTLAND WILL BE SCOTLAND

Devolution will increase democratic control, bring government
closer to the people, and recognise more fully the special
national characteristics of Scotland and Wales. Although the
Kilbrandon Commission expressed differing opinions on which
kind of devolution is best they were in no doubt that
devolution is needed.

> Government Reply to a Member
> of Parliament briefing on the
> 1975 "White Paper"

A decade of success and optimism ended in disappointment
with the defeat of the Scotland and Wales Bill. A March,
1979 Referendum asked Scots to vote on the possibility of a
National Assembly or Parliament with limited powers. Despite
much confusion over the referendum itself, a majority of
Scots approved the measure. However, a controversial rule
requiring 40% of the electorate defeated the Bill and left
many Scots with feelings of anger and betrayal. A new
militancy was born and left-wing nationalists began to plan
new strategies. The "79" Group represented one such radical
alternative. Scottish Nationalism seemed at a low ebb,
though many seeking an independent Scotland had not abandoned
hopes of self-rule under the aegis of the Labour Party.
Even so, a Scottish Labour Party was formed in 1976 to
gather more support for a Scottish Socialist Republic. Hugh
MacDiarmid's death in 1978 was a heavy blow to Scottish life
and politics. Many predicted hard struggles for survival into
the 1980's.

BOOKS AND PAMPHLETS

365. Alexander, K.J.W. The Political Economy of Change.
Oxford: Blackwell, 1975. 189pp.

Papers presented to Section F at the 1974 Annual
Meeting of the British Association for the Advancement
of Science. Four chapters in this book deal with
"change in the Scottish Context."

366. Alexander, K.J. W. "The Political Economy of Change."
In The Political Economy of Change. Oxford: Blackwell, 1975,
109-125.

Alexander is skeptical of North Sea oil as a panacea
for Scotland's political and economic ills.

367. Allen, C.H. "Chronology of Devolution 1885-1978." In
The Scottish Government Yearbook 1979, edited by H.M. Drucker,
204-207. Edinburgh: Paul Harris, 1978.

A chronology of Scottish devolution from the establishment
of the Secretary of State for Scotland post in 1885 to
the Scotland Bill of February, 1978.

368. Bogdanor, Vernon. Devolution. Oxford: Oxford U. Press,
1979. 246pp.

Sketches the history of Home Rule and devolution in
Ireland, Scotland, and Wales. Explains the Scotland
and Wales Bill. Views Scottish Nationalism since 1945
as it relates to the major political parties.

369. Bradley, A.W. "Devolution of Government in Britain-
Some Scottish Aspects." In Devolution, by Harry Calvert,
89-113. London: Professional Press, 1975.

Presents the structure of Scottish government and legal
system, the Kilbrandon Report, and the limits of
devolution within the United Kingdom.

370. Bradley, A.W., and Christie, D.J. The Scotland Act 1978.
Edinburgh: W. Green and Son, 1979.

Full text of the Scotland Act, annotated section by
section. Full discussion and notes.

371. Brand, Jack. The National Movement in Scotland. London:
Routledge and Kegan Paul, 1978. 300pp. bibl.

Brand offers comprehensive analysis of Scottish Nationalism, its nature, the rise of the Scottish National Party,
literary nationalism, the role of sport and the military
in nationalism. In-depth study of the various national
parties and their origins, doctrines, and mergers.

372. Butt, Philip A. "Devolution and Regionalism." In
Trends in British Politics Since 1945, edited by Chris Cook
and John Ramsden, 157-181. London: Macmillan, 1978.

    The authors argue that the responses by Westminster
    to demands for regional reform have been inadequate.

373. Calvert, Harry. Devolution. London: Professional
Press, 1975. 201pp.

    Papers presented at the Annual Colloquium of the UK
    National Committee on Comparative Law in Cardiff in
    Sept. 1974. Essays on devolution, the Kilbrandon
    Report, Belgium, France, and West Germany. Much
    attention given to Scottish Nationalism's impact
    on Britain and Europe.

374. Calvert, Harry. "Devolution in Perspective." In
Devolution, edited by Harry Calvert, 5-22. London:
Professional Press, 1975.

    Calvert defines the problem of devolution as one of
    redistribution of authority, and sees devolution as
    only one solution among many.

375. Calvert, Harry. "Who Wants Devolution?" In Devolution,
edited by Harry Calvert, 41-62. London: Professional Press,
1975.

    In-depth analysis of the popular attitudes to devolution.

376. Caporaso, James. "What is the New Nationalism or Is
There a New Nationalism?" In The New Nationalism: Implications
for Transatlantic Relations, edited by Werner Link and Werner
J. Feld, 6-22. Oxford: Pergamon, 1979.

    An objective presentation of the "new nationalism,"
    its dangers, its internal and domestic side. Caporaso
    finds this new nationalism less "bellicose and
    xenophobic" than supposed.

377. Carty, Tony., and Smith, Alexander M. Power and
Manoeuvrability. Edinburgh: Q Press, 1978. 185pp.

    The authors investigate the options possible to the
    small nations of the modern world. Using Scotland as an
    example, they study oil, politics, trade, money, etc.
    They conclude that small nations have many inherent
    disadvantages and advantages and believe that there
    can be important roles for smaller states in the
    international arena.

378.   Clarke, M.G. and Drucker, H.M. Our Changing Scotland:
a Yearbook of Scottish Government 1976-1977. Edinburgh:
Edinburgh University Student Publications Board, 1976.
154pp. bib.

    Chapters on devolution, unemployment, local government,
    the economics of independence and other topics.
    Excellent bibliography of items on Scottish politics
    from newspapers, magazines, and books.

379.   Cook, Chris, and Ramsden, John. Trends in British
Politics Since 1945. London: MacMillan, 1978. 197pp.

    Welsh and Scottish Nationalism are discussed at great
    length.

380.   Craig, F.W.S. Minor Parties at British Parliamentary
Elections 1885-1974. London: Macmillan, 1975. 147pp.

    Policies of parties, votes received, forfeited deposits,
    candidates, etc. Data given for the Scottish National
    Party and the Scottish Party. Such information is
    found in other sources, but the section on the
    Scottish National Party (pages 89-97) is especially
    useful.

381.   Craigie, Peter. "Industrial Relations." In The Radical
Approach: Papers on an Independent Scotland, edited by Gavin
Kennedy, 93-97. Edinburgh: Palingenesis Press, 1976.

    How should an independent Scotland handle industrial
    relations? Craigie hopes for a pragmatic and non-
    ideological approach that would eliminate exploitation
    and insure equal distribution without the waste and
    conflict so typical of British industrial relations
    as he finds them today.

382.   Currie, Andrew. "The Highland Problem." In The Radical
Approach: Papers on an Independent Scotland, edited by
        Gavin Kennedy, 33-46. Edinburgh: Palingenesis Press, 1976.

    Currie discusses Gaelic, transport, land reform, education,
    emigration, the impact of oil, the future of farming and
    fishing, and proposes solutions to these major problems
    in the Highlands.

383.   Daintith, Terence. "The Kilbrandon Report: Some
Comments." In Devolution, edited by Harry Calvert, 23-40.
London: Professional Press, 1975.

    A thorough discussion of the Kilbrandon Report, its
    importance, problems and limitations, especially its
    lack of civil rights provision.

384. Dalyell, Tam. Devolution: The End of Britain? London:
Jonathan Cape, 1977. 321pp.

   Dalyell, a Scot and Labour Party Member of Parliament,
   argues strongly against devolution or independence in
   Scotland and Wales. He researches at great length the
   history behind Home Rule and its current expression in
   Scotland. He believes much of the support for self-rule
   is based on faulty premises. He explains the origins
   and features of the Scotland and Wales Bill. He draws
   many parallels from the Irish experience. Concluding
   that there is a legitimate case for democratic reform,
   he offers several solutions that might prove satisfactory
   to Scots and English alike. A strong and careful argument
   against Scottish Nationalism.

385. Donaldson, Arthur. Whys of Scottish Nationalism.
Edinburgh: SNP Publications, 1976.

   A list of 39 questions on Scottish Nationalism: its
   history, aims, economic theories, position on civil
   liberties, Gaelic and Scots, wearing the kilt, etc.
   A useful primer on Scottish National Party policies.

386. Drucker, H.M. The Scottish Government Yearbook 1979.
Edinburgh: Paul Harris, 1978. 269pp.

   Contents include Highland land reform, the revolutionary
   left in Scotland, a chronology of devolution in Scotland,
   the Scotland Bill. Has excellent reference section and
   bibliography.

387. Donnachie, Ian. The Open University and Scottish
Devolution: Some Points for Discussion. 1976. 6pp.

   Donnachie thinks the Open University should preserve its
   present status within the United Kingdom, but should
   increase options for Scottish students, allowing for
   different social and cultural conditions prevailing in
   Scotland.

388. Esman, Milton. "Scottish Nationalism, North Sea Oil,
and the British Response." In Ethnic Conflict in the Western
World, edited by Milton Esman, 251-256. Ithaca: Cornell, 1977.

   Esman views the rise of Scottish Nationalism in the 70's.
   He thinks it is a response to several factors: visions
   of prosperity, relative deprivation, Britain's general
   decline, and others.

389. Ferguson, William. Scotland: 1689 to the Present.
Edinburgh: Oliver and Boyd, 1978. 470pp. bibl.

   A general history, touching on themes of nationality and
   nationalism.

390.   Foster, Charles R. "Trans-National Policy in a Sub-Regional Context: The Case for Scotland." In The New Nationalism: Implications for Transatlantic Relations, edited by Werner Link and Werner J. Feld, 119-125. Oxford: Pergamon, 1979.

Foster argues that "Scottish Nationalism is not a transitory phenomenon" but is a "prototype of a new type of limited ethnic-nationalism, radical yet non-violent." As a "sub-state," he sees great future influence for Scotland in British and European politics.

391.   Grant, John P., ed. Independence and Devolution: the Legal Implications for Scotland. Edinburgh: W. Green and Son, 1976. 233pp.

This work deals solely with the legal problems and possibilities of Scottish independence. Among the areas considered are tax and family law, criminal law, and international law. Many complex legal issues are examined.

392.   Grimond, Jo., and Neve, Brian. The Referendum. London: Rex Collings, 1975. 128pp.

Deals specifically with referendum; its uses, history, and importance to British democracy. This book, authored in part by Jo Grimond, Liberal Party Member of Parliament, is concerned mainly with the first national referendum on the question of Britain's entry into the Common Market, but also provides good background material on future referenda. Scottish and Welsh Nationalism are discussed vis a vis referendum.

393.   Harvie, Christopher. Scotland and Nationalism: Scottish Society and Politics, 1707-1977. London: Allen and Unwin, 1977. 318pp.

In this key work on Scottish Nationalism, Harvie writes on: "Political Nationalism 1707-1945," "Unionist Scotland," "The Intellectuals," and "Forward from Nationalism," and tries to account for the dynamic between nationalism and unionism in Scotland. Harvie sees devolution as no easy option, but one depending on English perceptions of democracy and centralization.

394. Hechter, Michael. Internal Colonialism: the Celtic
Fringe in British National Development, 1536-1966. Berkeley:
University of California Press, 1977. 361pp.

A complex sociological and theoretical study of the
Celtic "periphery" in British history and politics.
Several theories of colonialism are advanced. Parallels
are drawn with Black Nationalism in the USA.
Hechter discusses theories of ethnic change, and uses
graphs, tables, and statistics to reach an understanding
of inequalities in regional development and industrial
expansion. Thorough discussion of Scotland and Scottish
Nationalism. Hechter's conclusion provides important
insights into the future of nationalism in Britain and
elsewhere. Hechter's work is influential and is widely
discussed in Scotland.

395. Her Majesty's Stationery Office. Devolution: Financing
the Devolved Services. London: HMSO, 1977. 24pp.

This official government paper sets out the proposals
for financing devolved services in Scotland and Wales.
"White Paper."

396. Hutchison, David., ed. Headlines...the Media in Scotland.
Edinburgh: Edinburgh University, 1978. 112pp.

Essays on the Scottish press and its control and
influence. Other media investigated. The subject of
bias in the media is thoroughly explored. The book
concludes that the media has, on the whole, been hostile
or indifferent to Scottish Nationalism.

397. Kellas, James G. "Administering Scotland: a Critique
and Forward Look." In The Political Economy of Change, edited
by K.J.W. Alexander, 162-167. Oxford: Blackwell, 1975.

Notes contradictions between British and Scottish
requirements. Points to regions like Texas and Alberta
where wealth has been kept from oil exploration without
damage to federation.

398. Kerr, John. "The Media and Nationalism." In Headlines
...The Media in Scotland, edited by David Hutchison, 93-
102. Edinburgh: Edinburgh U. Student Publications Bureau,
1978.

Kerr dissects the reaction of Scotland's media to
Scottish Nationalism. He concludes that there was
much deliberate distortion and bias and that the press
was "basically hostile to nationalism."

399.   Lindsay, Isobel. "Nationalism, Community and Democracy." In The Radical Approach: Papers on an Independent Scotland, edited by Gavin Kennedy, 21-26. Edinburgh: Palingenesis Press, 1976.

Lindsay rejects the notion that nationalism is anything but a neutral term. The ingredients of nationalism are important. She presents the positive side of Scottish Nationalism as its insistence on true local democracy, opposition to centralized authority and imperialism, and its support for cultural liberation. Lindsay also emphasizes the concept of "community" and its role in Scotland's future.

400.   Link, Werner, and Feld, Werner J., eds. The New Nationalism: Implications for Transatlantic Relations. Oxford: Pergamon, 1979. 165pp.

Papers presented at the Annual Conference of the Committee on Atlantic Studies in Luxembourg in Sept. 1977. Defines "new nationalism" and its evidence in Quebec, Ireland, and Scotland.

401.   MacColla, Fionn. Too Long in this Condition. Thurso: John Humphries, n.d.   112pp.

Autobiography of Tom MacDonald. Much attention devoted to language and nationality., Small states are morally superior to large ones, he argues.

402.   McIntyre, John. "Devolving the Universities: Prospects and Problems." In Our Changing Scotland: A Yearbook of Scottish Government 1976-1977, edited by M.G. Clarke and H.M. Drucker, 87-97. Edinburgh: Edinburgh Student Publication Board, 1976.

A clarification of the problems and solutions of the finance of Scotland's universities.

403.   MacKay, D.I. "North Sea Oil and the Scottish Economy." In The Political Economy of Change, edited by K.J.W. Alexander, 126-150. Oxford: Blackwell, 1975.

The direct and indirect effects of oil on future Scottish politics, concluding that the indirect benefits of North Sea oil may promote faster and surer economic growth in Scotland.

404.   MacKay, D.I. and MacKay, G.A. The Political Economy of North Sea Oil. London: Martin Robertson, 1975. 193pp.

Oil and the United Kingdom, geology of North Sea oil, economic effects, social effects, land policy and employment. See especially, chapter 8: "The Political Economy of North Sea Oil," which touches on the economics of devolution and independence.

405.   Mackay, Donald., ed. <u>Scotland 1980: the Economics of Self-Government</u>. Edinburgh: Q Press, 1977. 211pp.

The work states: "The 13 contributors argue neither for nor against self-government-they simply assume a self-governing Scotland in 1980 and consider the implications." Topics range from North Sea oil and gas to the cost of defending a nation of six million people. Notes and references direct the reader to further resources and all arguments are supported by tables, graphs, and charts.

406.   Mackay, Donald I., ed. <u>Scotland: the Framework for Change</u>. Edinburgh: Paul Harris, 1979. 196pp.

Given a Scottish Assembly, Mackay argues for its likely role, its relation to Westminster, its powers, and the theoretical and practical difficulties an independent Scotland might encounter.

407.   Mackintosh, John P. <u>The Government and Politics of Great Britain</u>. London: Hutchinson, 1977. 244pp. bibl.

An enquiry into all aspects of British political life, including Parliament, the office of the Prime Minister, Trade Unions, the Constitution, and many others. Devolution, the Scottish National Party, regionalism, and related topics are also discussed.

408.   Maclean, Colin. <u>The Crown and the Thistle: the Nature of Nationhood</u>. Edinburgh: Scottish Academic Press, 1979. 160pp.

An analysis of nationhood. See especially, "Language and Nationhood," by Randolph Quirk, and "Nation and Nationalism," by Neil MacCormick.

409.   Maxwell, Stephen. "Beyond Democracy." In <u>The Radical Approach: Papers on an Independent Scotland</u>, edited by Gavin Kennedy, 7-20. Edinburgh: Palingenesis Press, 1976.

Maxwell argues that the Scottish National Party can no longer be an "umbrella" party that caters to all who share the common goal of Scottish independence. Instead, it should discard stale and conservative ideas for truly radical ones and should aim for "radical democracy" with strong support from the working class.

410.   Mercer, John. <u>Scotland: the Devolution of Power</u>. London: John Calder, 1978. 250pp.

Scotland's quest for self-rule since 1707. Proposals of all parties are explored with regard to devolution, federalism, and complete independence. Mercer sees need for radical change to true democracy and not a mere transfer of power.

411. Naughtie, James. "The Scotland Bill in the House of Commons." In The Scottish Government Yearbook 1979, edited by H.M. Drucker, 16-35. Edinburgh: Paul Harris, 1978.

   A concise account of the Scotland Bill, its origins, the opposition to it, the compromises that created it, and, finally, how the now infamous "40% Rule" came about. An excellent explanation of a complicated subject.

412. Purves, David. "Environmental Policy in an Independent Scotland." In The Radical Approach: Papers on an Independent Scotland, edited by Gavin Kennedy, 88-92. Edinburgh: Palingenesis Press, 1976.

   Urges a vital Scottish Ministry of the Environment or an Environmental Protection Agency to formulate policies on population, agriculture, fisheries, forestry, and other areas that the author views as suffering most under Westminster rule.

413. Ronen, Dov. The Quest for Self-Determination. New Haven: Yale University Press, 1979. 144pp.

   A study of the concept of self-determination of nations. Examples and case studies given. Chapter 4: "Four Examples: The Scots, Biafra, Palestine, and South Africa." Historical and philosophical treatment. Includes select bibliography.

414. Scottish Liberal Party. Scottish Self-Government. London: John Calder, 1976. 40pp.

   Statement of the Liberal Party's commitment to devolution for Scotland. Federalism within the United Kingdom is the ideal. Federalism is presented in its practical and legal aspects.

415. Seton-Watson, Hugh. Nations and States: an inquiry into the origins of nations and the politics of nationalism. London: Methuen, 1977. 563pp. bibl.

   Detailed study of all facets of nationalism in Europe, Asia, and Africa. Scotland is discussed. Traces influence of class, ideology, and race on nationalism. Compares various national movements. Clarifies notions of "state" and "nation." Lengthy bibliography.

416. Simpson, David. "Economic Growth in Scotland: Theory and Experience." In The Political Economy of Change, edited by K.J. W. Alexander, 151-161. Oxford: Blackwell, 1975.

   Traces decline of Scottish economy from 1870 to present. Simpson projects future growth of the economy on the condition of better leadership, income distribution, access to markets, and more self-rule for Scotland.

417. Smallwood, C.R. and Mackay, D. "The Economics of Independence." In Our Changing Scotland: a Yearbook of Scottish Government, 1976-1977, edited by M.G. Clarke and H.M. Drucker, 98-107. Edinburgh: E.U.S.P.B., 1976.

Smallwood discusses oil, monetary union, balance of payments, exchange rates, and inflation, and argues for devolution but not independence for Scotland. MacKay says that North Sea oil will not buy prosperity but may provide the time for policies and solutions to emerge.

418. Smith, Anthony D.S. Nationalism in the Twentieth Century. Oxford: Martin Robertson, 1979. 257pp. bibl.

A virtual encyclopedia of modern nationalism. Thorough in every respect, with several pages devoted to Scottish Nationalism. Pertinent chapters include "Communist Nationalisms," and "Ethnic Resurgence in the West." Excellent select bibliography.

419. Smout, Christopher. "The Scottish Indentity." In The Future of Scotland, edited by Robert Underwood, 11-21. London: Croom Helm, 1977.

Smout finds that there is a true Scottish identity, but not in a racial sense. Major changes since World War II make the old Union unwieldy, but Smout cautions in comparing Scotland with other nations or regions when discussing independence.

420. Underwood, Robert., ed. The Future of Scotland. London: Croom Helm, 1977. 181pp.

Collection of essays on issues confronting an independent Scotland. These issues include natural resources, energy, diet, health care, education, industry, and defence.

421. Webb, Keith. The Growth of Nationalism in Scotland. Glasgow: Molendinar Press, 1977. 147pp. bibl.

Overview of Scottish Nationalism from the 17th century. Emphasis on key individuals and significant parties. Religion's influence on Scottish Nationalism is explored. Webb projects future events based on his study of the past. Good general bibliography is included.

422. Zwerin, Michael. A Case for the Balkanization of Practically Everyone: the New Nationalism. London: Wildwood, 1976. 190pp.

Modern European examples of nationalism: Occitan, Basque, Welsh, Breton, Catalan, and more, with an inclusion of the Scottish Nationalist Manifesto.

ARTICLES

423. Bayne, Ian. "English-ridden, capitalist-ridden, landlord-ridden Scotland." Crann Tara (Autumn 1978): 14-16.

A view of the struggle for Scottish self-rule from 1882-1924, concentrating on the reasons for the defeat of the many popular Home Rule Bills. The title of the article comes from a famous speech by James Maxton, popular orator and member of the Labour Party.

424. Bayne, Ian. "English-ridden, capitalist-ridden, landlord-ridden Scotland." Crann Tara (Winter 1978): 18-19.

Key events from 1927-1967 in Scots quest for independence.

425. Boothby, Jennifer. "Nationalism and Freedom." Sgian Dubh 11 (October 1975): 5-6.

Contrasts the Celtic nations' notion of freedom with Nazism and concludes that English imperialism has more in common with Nazism than does Scottish Nationalism.

426. Bold, Alan. "A National Community." Scotia Review (April 1976): 2-6.

Scots poet Bold observes how attached the English are to an English identity, and believes the Scots have a similar right to define themselves.

427. Brand, Jack. "The SNP: from Protest to Nationalism." New Society (November 11, 1975): 416-418.

How the SNP managed to increase its vote from 2% to 30% in ten years. Nationalist vote should be studied as part of a complex and permanent phenomenon, argues Brand.

428. Cavan, Ted. "Sorting out the Myths." Question (May 13, 1977): 4.

Some myths surrounding the idea of clan gatherings and the fallacy of the idea of a "proto-Socialist Scotland".

429. Cornford, James. "The English Dilemma." Question (June 1977): 7.

Article centers on how the English would benefit from devolution because it would bring democracy to England.

430. Currie, Andrew. "The S.N.P. and Participation."
Question (April 1976): 8-10.

> Currie believes that the S.N.P. offers a unique
> opportunity for left and right to join in a common
> cause-Scottish independence.

431. Frowein, Dr. Jochen. "Devolution: satisfying a
minority." Journal of the Law Society of Scotland 22
(July 1977): 237-299.

> Dr. Frowein finds lessons from German devolution and
> from the Crown Colonies to suggest to those seeking
> legal interpretations of Scottish self-government.
> He discusses the need for protection of minority
> rights.

432. Gibson, Peter. "The S.N.P. and Housing." Question
(June 1976): 8-10.

> A criticism of the Scottish National Party's housing
> policies, with suggestions for a more radical program.

433. Gibson, Rob. "It's Scotland's Soil." Crann Tara
(Spring 1978): 8-9.

> A summary of the land policy of the Scottish National
> Party.

434. Gibson, Rob. "Left, Right, Left, Right." Calgacus
1 (Winter 1975): 14-16.

> Appraisal of Scottish National Party successes in the
> October, 1974 General Election. Gibson urges Scottish
> Nationalists to complete the radical social reforms
> which eluded the Labour Party for so many years.

435. Hall, Peter. "The Geographical Puzzle of the Regions."
New Society (July 1, 1976): 6-8.

> Hall discusses the problems of British regionalism.
> He believes Scottish Nationalism is very much a
> product of geography.

436. Harvie, Christopher. "The Road from 1885." Question
(April 1976): 5-7.

> Draws parallels between Scottish situation and Gladstone
> and Irish Home Rule. Harvie argues that bureaucracy
> and centralization resulted when true radicals like
> Joseph Chamberlain didn't succeed with their policies.

437. Hunter, James. "The Lessons of History." Question
(May 1976): 8-11.

   Compares Scottish Nationalism with Irish Home Rule of
   the 1870's and 80's. He believes that cultural
   nationalism must also be tied to some specific social
   and economic reforms in order to be successful.

438. Kennedy, Gavin. "Defence in Scotland." Question
(June 1976): 4-5.

   Scotland's strategic position in Britain and Europe
   forces careful thinking about the defence policies of
   an independent Scotland.

439. Lenman, Bruce. "The Scottish Universities and Devolution."
Scotia Review (Summer 1977): 11-20.

   Lenman attacks what he considers "neo-colonialism" in
   the staffing of Scottish universities.

440. Lynn, Richard. "The Sociobiology of Nationalism."
New Society (July 1, 1976): 11-14.

   Lynn suggests that only "sociobiology can offer a
   convincing theory of nationalism," linking nationalism
   to survival and evolution.

441. MacDonald, Jack S. "Home Truths for Dreamy Clansmen."
The Patriot (April/May, 1977): 1-2.

   A challenge to the visitors to clan gatherings to
   confront the real Scotland of poverty, slums, ill health,
   high unemployment, and oppression.

442. MacInnes, Violet. "The Dawn of a New Era for Scotland?"
The Patriot (Feb./March 1976): 2-4.

   The significance of the founding of the Scottish Labour
   Party by Labour Member of Parliament Jim Sillars.

443. Mackintosh, John P. "The Trouble with Stephen Maxwell."
Question (April 15, 1977): 5.

   Mackintosh, in answer to Maxwell and others, argues that
   Scots can be both "British" and "Scottish" and that
   small nations like Scotland are too much at the mercy
   of world economics to be independent in any meaningful
   way.

444. Maxwell, Stephen. "Anglo-Saxon Attitudes." Question
(October 1976): 3.

   Maxwell tackles a dilemma: how to assimilate the best
   of English attitudes while resisting political
   domination by those same attitudes and influences.

445. Maxwell, Stephen. "Can Scotland's Political Myths Be
Broken?" Question (November 1976): 5.

    Denied political independence, Scotland has created
    myths-the "Unionist Myth," "The Loyal Scot," "The Red
    Clyde," and so on. Maxwell argues that any Scottish
    Nationalist program must challenge these myths and
    build policies based on truth and realism.

446. Maxwell, Stephen. "Politics and Culture." Question
(April 1, 1977): 4-5.

    Asks why Scottish political revival has had so little
    impact on the arts. Maxwell concludes that Scotland's
    true case for cultural independence has yet to be made.

447. Maxwell, Stephen. "Scotland and Quebec." Question
(March 4, 1977): 9-10.

    Parallels are drawn between Quebec and Scotland.
    Maxwell concludes that both are at comparable economic
    and cultural stages.

448. Maxwell, Stephen. "Scotland's Foreign Policy."
Question (Sept. 1976): 5-7.

    Maxwell considers the opinion that an independent
    Scotland would soon be at the mercy of NATO, the CIA,
    foreign multinationals, etc. He doubts that a
    complex and democratic Scotland would very easily
    submit to outside controls such as these.

449. Nairn, Tom. "The English Dilemma." Question (Feb. 1977):
3-4.

    A subtle analysis of English racism and nationality.

450. Nairn, Tom. "The New Exiles." Question (April 1977):7.

    A sympathetic treatment of English intellectuals living
    in Scotland, and their mistakes in equating the Scottish
    desire for independence with anti-English racism or
    with provincialism.

451. Nairn, Tom. "The Radical Approach." Question (July 1976):
8-11.

    Nairn finds that the old quarrels about socialism and
    nationalism must give way to new and radical ways of
    looking at socialism and nationalism.

452. Reid, George. "A State of Flux." Question (Feb. 1976):
4-5.

    Considers the possible political options after
    Scotland's independence is achieved.

453. Rose, Richard. "Scotland in Perspective." _Question_ (January 1976): 5-6.

An outsider's view of Scotland: a diverse country, no apparent unity, and not able, even with self-rule, to reduce dependence on England, the EEC, OPEC, etc.

454. Rose, Richard. "What is Scotland Voting About?" _New Society_ (Feb. 1979): 294-296.

Analysis of the referendum of March, 1979. Rose explains the reasons for confusion about the issues.

455. Smout, T.C. "The Historical Separateness of the Scots." _New Society_ (July 1, 1976): 8-11.

Smout writes that Scots no longer have much to gain from continued association with England, especially after the decline of Britain's economy. He also thinks that most Scots would prefer to maintain the British connection if they are treated with respect and fairness by Westminster.

456. Wares, Roy. "The Canadian-Scottish Connection." _Crann Tara_ (Autumn 1978): 8-10.

Scotland vis a vis England, and Canada vis a vis the USA, with comparisons also drawn between Quebec and Scotland.

457. Weightman, Gavin. "Scottish Power." _New Society_ (Feb. 9, 1978): 314-318.

Weightman outlines the defects of the Scotland Bill, criticizing its lack of key powers in the area of heavy industry and consumer protection.

458. White, Stephen, and Dickson, J. "The Future of the SNP." _New Society_ (Sept. 23, 1976): 663-664.

A survey of managers and workers in the west of Scotland. The survey studies the voting patterns of those who would vote for the Scottish National Party. The authors conclude that the SNP would not survive self-government and would lose its support to Labour and Conservative.

6.

SCOTTISH NATIONALISM: SOCIALISM AND INTERNATIONALISM

I would ask no greater job in life than to make English-
ridden, capitalist-ridden, land-owner ridden Scotland into
the free Scottish Socialist Commonwealth.
                              James Maxton
                              St. Andrew's Hall, Glasgow
                              1924

Perhaps more than the socialists of any region or country,
Scots socialists have clarified the relationship of socialism
and nationalism. Many have sought to forge links between the
small states of Europe and the Third World, while attacking
the imperialism masked as internationalism of the great
powers. Actually, left-wing nationalism has a long history
in Scotland, and pre-dates Keir Hardie and the Independent
Labour Party. Later, James Connolly, John MacLean, Hugh
MacDiarmid and others argued strongly in support of small-
nation socialism, and hoped that this might hasten the
destruction of the British Empire. This tradition is
continued today by Tom Nairn, Stephen Maxwell, Dr. James
Young and many more Scots who see no contradiction between
nationalism and true internationalism. Anyone who still
believes that Scottish Nationalists are all "Tartan Tories"
is not doing justice to the richness of Scottish left-wing
nationalist thought. This synthesis between socialism and
nationalism may be Scotland's lasting contribution to
European political thought.

BOOKS AND PAMPHLETS

459. Bell, Tom. John MacLean: a Fighter for Freedom.
Glasgow: Communist Party, Scottish Committee, 1944. 173pp.

A mainly political biography of MacLean with only a
short discussion of his Scottish republicanism or of
his desire for Scottish independence.

460. Broom, John. John MacLean. Loanhead: MacDonald, 1973.
207pp.

A standard biography of John MacLean, with one whole
chapter devoted to MacLean's reasons for a "Scottish
Worker's Republican Party."

461. Brown, Gordon., ed. The Red Paper on Scotland.
Edinburgh: Edinburgh University Student Publications Bureau,
1975. 368pp.

Termed a "Socialist contribution to the present debate
about Scotland's future." Possibly the most important
and influential work on Scottish Nationalism in the 70's.
Topics: Ireland, industrial democracy, North Sea oil,
socialism, nationalism and internationalism, and many
more. Useful footnotes and references.

462. Brown, Oliver. Arms and the Men. Glasgow: Robert
Thomson, 1943. 32pp.

A view of World War II from a Scottish socialist position.
Brown argues that the war came about from abuses of
nationalism and not nationalism per se.

463. Burnett, Ray. "Socialists and the SNP." In The Red
Paper on Scotland, edited by Gordon Brown, 108-124.
Edinburgh: EUSPB, 1975.

An indictment of the SNP by a socialist, claiming that
the SNP can't be a true separatist party because of its
bourgeois composition.

464. Connolly, James. "The Friends of Small Nationalities."
In Socialism and Nationalism: A Selection from the Writings
of James Connolly, edited by Desmond Ryan, 148-151. Dublin:
Sign of the Three Candles, 1948.

Connolly condemns the hypocrisy of World War I, fought
for the rights of small nations, while Ireland and other
small nations were being oppressed.

465. Connolly, James. "The Language Movement." In Socialism and Nationalism: A Selection from the Writings of James Connolly, edited by Desmond Ryan, 58-64. Dublin: Sign of the Three Candles, 1948.

> Language revival can be a key feature of political freedom, argues Connolly, for oppression of a language and culture results in slavish and dependent attitudes in a people. This makes them too docile for radical change.

466. Connolly, James. "Socialism and Irish Nationalism." In Socialism and Nationalism: A Selection from the Writings of James Connolly, edited by Desmond Ryan, 33-37. Dublin, Sign of the Three Candles, 1948.

> Connolly sees nationalism as a means to an end, not an end in itself. Nationalism mustn't lose sight of its goals: true equality and socialism.

467. Connolly, James. "Socialism and Nationalism." In Socialism and Nationalism: A Selection from the Writings of James Connolly, edited by Desmond Ryan, 22-27. Dublin, Sign of the Three Candles, 1948.

> Connolly defends nationalism on socialist grounds, but also concludes that nationalism without socialism is not worth fighting for.

468. Davis, Horace B. Nationalism and Socialism: Marxist and Labour Theories of Nationalism to 1917. NY: Monthly Review, 1967. 258pp.

> Theories of nationality in Marx, Engels, and Lenin. Nationalism and internationalism investigated. Important chapter entitled: "The Working Class and Nationalism."

469. Davies, Noelle. Connolly of Ireland. Caernarfon: Swiddfa'r Blaid, 1946. 59pp.

> Davies' biography centers around Connolly's significance to national movements in Wales and elsewhere. Davies also discusses the importance of Connolly's blend of nationalism and socialism, most of which also applies to Scotland.

470. Deasy, Joseph. The Teachings of James Connolly. Dublin: New Books, 1968. 14pp.

> Connolly's life and political theories, with space devoted to Connolly's nationalism and socialism. Deasy sees Connolly's blend of nationalism and socialism as orthodox Marxism.

471. Drucker, Henry. Breakaway: the Scottish Labour Party.
Edinburgh: Edinburgh U. Student Publications Bureau, 1977.
157pp.

Chronicles the formation of the Scottish Labour Party
in 1976. He outlines the reasons for its revolt against
the Labour Party. He explains its devotion to socialism
and nationalism and its goal of an "independent Socialist
Scotland." Appendix: "The Scottish Labour Party: Statement of Aims."

472. Earle, Edward M., ed. Nationalism and Internationalism.
NY: Columbia U. Press, 1950. 510pp.

A thorough discussion of nationalism and internationalism
through examples ranging from Hegel to Jim Larkin, from
Scandinavia to Ireland, but not touching specifically
on Scottish Nationalism.

473. Edwards, Owen Dudley. "Scotland: Lessons from Ireland."
In Red Paper on Scotland, edited by Gordon Brown, 304-316.
Edinburgh: EUSPB, 1975.

Edwards, himself Irish, hopes that Scotland's quest for
independence will take Ireland's mistakes into account.
Religious bigotry and parochial politics should be
avoided and James Connolly's blend of a small-nation
socialism with nationalism might serve as a model for
Scotland.

474. Edwards, Owen Dudley. "Socialism or Nationalism?" In
The Radical Approach, edited by Gavin Kennedy, 98-109.
Edinburgh: Q Press, 1976.

Edwards reconciles the SNP's positive nationalism with
its positive socialism and proposes a "true, radical
and real independence" for Scotland within a socialist
framework.

475. Ellis, P. Beresford., ed. James Connolly: Selected
Writings. NY: Monthly Review Press, 1974. 317pp. bibl.

Chronology of Connolly's life. See especially: "Socialism
and Nationalism," "The Friends of Small Nationalities,"
and "The Language Movement."

476. Ferry, Alex. "Industrial Democracy and Worker's
Control." In Red Paper on Scotland, edited by Gordon Brown,
98-107. Edinburgh: EUSPB, 1975.

Industrial democracy, worker's participation, and
worker's control are all necessary in a truly free
Scotland, argues Ferry.

477. Firn, John. "External Control and Regional Policy." In The Red Paper on Scotland, edited by Gordon Brown, 153-169. Edinburgh: EUSPB, 1975.

Because political and economic control must be very widespread in Scotland, Firn recommends careful investigation of that control in order to plan effectively for a free Scotland.

478. Foster, John. "Capitalism and the Scottish Nation." In The Red Paper on Scotland, edited by Gordon Brown, 141-152. Edinburgh: EUSPB, 1975.

National parliaments can alone break the grip of what Foster terms "monopoly capitalism" in Britain. Wales and Scotland, concludes Foster, must thus use independence to put an end to exploitation in all of Britain.

479. Gow, David. "Devolution and Democracy." In The Red Paper on Scotland, edited by Gordon Brown, 58-68. Edinburgh: EUSPB, 1975.

Gow sees Scotland as an ideal nation for autonomy. It could, he hopes, avoid centralization and distribute wealth and resources on socialist principles, thus becoming an example of true democracy to the rest of Europe.

480. Greaves, C. Desmond. The Life and Times of James Connolly. NY: International Publishers, 1971. 448pp. bibl.

Biography. Gives valuable new information about Connolly's birth in Edinburgh and on his formative years in Scotland. Much attention given to Connolly's ideas and influence.

481. Hunter, James. "The Crofter, the Laird and the Agrarian Socialist: the Highland Land Question in the 1970's." In The Scottish Government Yearbook, 48-60. Edinburgh: Paul Harris, 1978.

Hunter writes that the central task of an independent Scotland is land reform. He examines the 1976 Crofting Reform Act. Hunter explains the complexities of land ownership and registration in the Highlands.

482. Kendall, Walter. The Revolutionary Movement in Britain 1900-1921: the Origins of British Communism. London: Weidenfeld, 1969. 453pp. bibl.

See chapter 17: "John MacLean and the Communist Party Great Britain" for a discussion of MacLean's notion of a Scottish Worker's Republic and of Scottish independence. Useful work for an understanding of MacLean's ideas.

483.   Kirkwood, Colin. "Community Democracy." In The Red Paper on Scotland, edited by Gordon Brown, 85-97. Edinburgh: EUSPB, 1975.

    Kirkwood explains how tenant associations, community newspapers, action groups, etc. could function in a small nation.

484.   Kennedy, Gavin., ed. The Radical Approach: Papers on an Independent Scotland. Edinburgh: Palingenesis Press, 1976, 109pp.

    Various contributors, many of them socialists and/or nationalists. Topics: democracy, housing, North Sea oil, health care, Orkney and Shetland, the environment, and more. A realistic approach to Scottish independence and the problems it would bring, and possible solutions to those problems.

485.   Lenin, V.I. "London International Socialist Congress of 1896." In Selected Works: a One Volume Selection of Lenin's Most Essential Writings. London: Lawrence and Wishart, 1969, 166-168.

    Lenin's recognition of the rights of small nations to self-determination, and "the particular urgency of this demand" under imperialist rule in Britain.

486.   Lenin, V.I. "Marxism and Proudhonism on the National Question." In Selected Works: a One Volume Selection of Lenin's Most Essential Writings. London: Lawrence and Wishart, 1969, 162-163.

    Lenin, explaining Marx, says here that no free nation can oppress another nation and that all nationalist movements are "progressive when they are non-imperialist." He concludes that Ireland thus had the right to throw off English rule.

487.   Lenin, V.I. "The Second Congress of the Communist International July 19-August 7, 1920. Report of the Commission on the National and the Colonial Questions." In Selected Works: a One Volume Selection of Lenin's Most Essential Writings. London: Lawrence and Wishart, 1969, 602-606.

    Lenin makes his famous distinction between "oppressed" and "oppressor" nations. "Oppressed" nations have the right to national independence in order to halt that oppression. This work is of particular relevance to left-wing Scottish Nationalism.

488. Lenin, V.I. Selected Works: A One Volume Selection of
Lenin's Most Essential Writings. London: Lawrence and
Wishart, 1969. 798pp.

 Several pages devoted to the self-determination of
 nations, and to justified nationalism. See chapter:
 "Socialist Revolution and the Right of Nations to
 Determination."

489. Lenin, V.I. "Three Types of Countries with Respect to
the Self-Determination of Nations." In Selected Works: a One
Volume Selection of Lenin's Most Essential Writings.London:
Lawrence and Wishart, 1969, 163-164.

 Lenin outlines the cases where the working classes
 should demand Home Rule for their own and for other
 nations. "Semi-colonial" countries must demand national
 liberation for their people.

490. McGrath, John. "Scotland: Up Against It." In The Red
Paper on Scotland, edited by Gordon Brown, 134-140.
Edinburgh: EUSPB, 1975.

 McGrath argues that a truly independent Scotland must
 be socialist and internationalist, and must resist all
 domination by outside agencies. Change must be radical
 or Scotland will have the same problems now facing her.
 McGrath adds that a free Scotland would no longer aid
 in the persecution of other nations and cultures.

491. Maxwell, Stephen. The Case for Left-Wing Nationalism.
SNP 79 Group Paper, No. 6. 1981. 24pp.

 Maxwell examines the critical weaknesses of organized
 Scottish Nationalism and feels that the urban working
 class must be one in their support for Scottish
 independence. Maxwell argues that Scotland's social
 ills demand a radical socialism that goes beyond current
 Labour Party policy. He urges the Scottish National
 Party "to establish itself as the radical Scottish
 alternative to the Labour Party."

492. Milton, Nan., ed. In the Rapids of Revolution: Essays
articles and letters 1902-1923. London: Allison and Busby,
1978. 256pp.

 The writings of John MacLean, edited by his daughter.
 Of special interest is chapter 11, "The Scottish Worker's
 Republic." Contains many references to MacLean's belief
 in an independent Scottish socialist republic.

493. Milton, Nan. John MacLean. London: Pluto Press, 1973.
318pp.

A standard biography of John MacLean by his daughter.

494. Mulholland, Robert. Scotland's Freedom Struggle:
Political, Social, and Cultural Aspects of the 1970's.
Alva: Crann Tara, 1978. 151pp.

Short articles taken from the Connolly Association's
Irish Democrat, from 1971-1977. The pieces deal with
nationalism and socialism, Ireland and Scotland, Celtic
Marxism, Scotland's languages and the importance of
Gaelic, and left-wing republicanism.

495. Nairn, Tom. "Old Nationalism and New Nationalism." In
The Red Paper on Scotland, edited by Gordon Brown, 22-57.
Edinburgh: EUSPB, 1975.

Nairn sees Scottish Nationalism as a new force that
requires new analysis. Its socialist and internationalist
nature must also be considered. He gives a detailed
interpretation of true internationalism.

496. Niven, Bill. "Regional Policy and the Scottish
Assembly." In The Red Paper on Scotland, edited by Gordon
Brown, 214-222. Edinburgh: EUSPB, 1975.

Niven suggests that Scotland should prepare itself for
the major changes that independence will bring and
should begin to modify existing institutions to that
end. He concentrates on trade unions and similar
organizations.

496a. Ryan, Desmond, ed. Socialism and Nationalism: a
Selection from the Writings of James Connolly. Dublin: The
Sign of the Three Candles, 1948. 211pp.

Writings have a bearing on Scottish Nationalism.
"Socialism and Nationalism", "The Language Movement",
and "Socialism and Irish Nationalism".

496b. Salmond, Alex. "Introduction." In The Scottish
Industrial Resistance, edited by Alex Salmond, 1-4.
79 Group Paper No. 7, 1982.

Salmond urges the Scottish National Party to support
civil disobedience in defence of Scottish jobs and to
take a more active role in defending the interests of
Scottish workers.

497.   Scott, John, and Hughes, Michael. "Finance Capital and the Upper Classes." In The Red Paper on Scotland, edited by Gordon Brown, 170-186. Edinburgh: EUSPB, 1975.

The authors argue that Scotland is dominated by international capital and must opt for an independence that will end that domination.

498.   Scottish Worker's Republican Party. Manifesto of the Scottish Worker's Republican Party. Glasgow: SWRP, 1925. 10pp.

Manifesto of the Party founded by John MacLean. It urges Scottish workers not to support Britain's empire nor to be "Empire Socialists." Instead, Scottish workers should support an independent Scotland and a worker's republic. The SWRP's motto: "Scotland for the Scottish Workers, the World for the World's Workers."

499.   Sillars, Jim. "Scottish Resistance." In The Scottish Industrial Resistance, edited by Alex Salmond, 79 Group Paper No. 7, 1982.

Explains the SNP campaign for industrial resistance. Sillars foresees much industrial unrest in the 1980's and believes Scottish Nationalists must ally with Scotland's workers and give them as much support as possible.

500.   Smith, Peter. "The Political Economy of North Sea Oil." In The Red Paper on Scotland, edited by Gordon Brown, 187-213. Edinburgh: EUSPB, 1975.

Smith contends that North Sea oil presents a paradox for Scotland and Home Rule. Nationalism would still leave the oil in USA and international hands, but Scotland could not manage the oil on her own.

501.   Tait, Bob. "The Left, the SNP and Oil." In The Red Paper on Scotland, edited by Gordon Brown, 125-133. Edinburgh: EUSPB, 1975.

The SNP should be seen as a progressive party, Tait writes, because it will hasten radical changes, including industrial democracy and civil rights.

502.   Toner, Pat. "Victory at Lee Jeans." In The Scottish Industrial Resistance, edited by Alex Salmond, 11-12. 79 Group Paper, No. 7, 1982.

Toner views an SNP involvement in the Lee Jeans occupation at the Greenock plant in 1981 as a new era of Scottish Nationalist concern for the Scottish working class.

503. Williamson, Neil. "Ten Years After-the Revolutionary Left in Scotland." In The Scottish Government Yearbook 1979, 61-77. Edinburgh: Paul Harris, 1978.

    Williamson summarizes the development, since 1968, of the Socialist Worker's Party, the International Marxist Group, the Worker's Revolutionary Party, and the Communist Party. In each case, he outlines the official party position on Scottish independence.

504. Young, James. "The Rise of Scottish Socialism." In The Red Paper on Scotland, edited by Gordon Brown, 282-288. Edinburgh: EUSPB, 1975.

    Young counters the myth of Scottish working class inertia. He argues that the Scottish labour movement has always been to the left of English labour, but unfortunately for Scottish self-government, has channelled much of its radicalism into non-political activities.

505. Young, James D. The Rousing of the Scottish Working Class. London: Croom Helm, 1979. 242pp. bibl.

    Dr. Young provides excellent analysis of the relationship between socialism and nationalism, and of Home Rule and the Scottish working class. See especially, Chapter 5: "The Rise of Scottish Socialism and National Identity 1880-1900" and chapter 7: "John MacLean, the Scottish Literary Renaissance and the Modern World, 1914-1931," Lengthy notes and bibliography.

506. Young, James D. The Scottish National Question and Labour History. n.d. 23pp.

    Pamphlet tackles the question of whether or not Scottish Nationalism is a progressive force. Young first contrasts the Communist Party Great Britain policy with that of MacLean's Scottish Worker's Republican Party. He notes the "monolithic tradition of proletarian universalism" in Scotland which makes it especially difficult for nationalists to endorse socialism and still be taken seriously by the Labour Party and by the labour movement. Young concludes that an independent Scotland would hardly be reactionary, but instead, might possibly become the "first democratic socialist society in Western Europe."

507. Young, Ronald. "What Sort of Overgovernment?" In The Red Paper on Scotland, edited by Gordon Brown, 69-84. Edinburgh: EUSPB, 1975.

    Young notes the fallacy of believing small government means efficient government by pointing to the corruption and inefficiency of local government in Scotland. Politicians desiring Scottish independence, argues Young, should study the faults of local government first.

ARTICLES

508. Ashton, Jack. "Scotland Now." Scottish Marxist (Winter 1978): 11-16.

Ashton, Scottish Secretary of the Communist Party, stresses the Communist Party's support of devolution or independence, but only if the result is an end to exploitation within Scotland as well as from without.

509. Bayne, Ian. "The Radical Heritage of Scottish Nationalism." Crann Tara (Summer 1978): 8-9.

Bayne refutes the "Tartan Tory" image of Scots Nationalism by placing it firmly within a strong radical tradition in Scotland.

510. Broom, John. "The Kind of Scotland I Want." Catalyst 1 (Autumn 1968): 10-11.

John MacLean's biographer imagines an ideal Scotland: a Constitutional Socialist Republic with a Social Credit system, with sweeping powers in agrarian reform, and a nation working for international peace.

511. Brown, Oliver. "Dialogues for the times: nationalist and socialist." Scots Independent (November 1931): 13.

Playing devil's advocate, Brown acknowledges that nationalism has a "spiritual force" often lacking in socialism.

512. Brown, Oliver. "Duty of Internationalism." National Weekly 4 (May 3, 1952): 1.

Finding the 1914 endorsement of war by socialists in most European countries as a betrayal of true internationalism, Brown argues that internationalism can only develop from a true nationalism which Scots must strive for. He concludes: "We are not British
                                        We are Scots
                                        We are Europeans
                                        We are Citizens of the
                                        World."

513. Brown, Oliver. "English Rulers Attack on Republicans." Scots Socialist (June 1941): 1.

A report of the police raids on the Scottish Socialist offices during World War II, and on the intimidation of socialists and nationalists in Scotland.

514. Brown, Oliver. "Keir Hardie: Scottish Nationalist and International Socialist." Scots Socialist (Sept. 1940): 2-3.

Brown shows several successful examples of the blending of nationalism and internationalism, citing Connolly, Ataturk, Nehru, and Keir Hardie.

515.   Brown, Oliver. "Leninism and Nationalism." Scots
Independent (November 1933): 14.

   Brown applies Lenin's theories on self-determination to
   Scotland and believes Scottish Nationalism is justified
   by Marx and Lenin.

516.   Brown, Oliver. "Nationalism and Socialism: Antagonism
or Co-operation?" Scots Independent (December 1937): 14.

   Scotland and Marxist views of nationalism.

517.   Brown, Oliver. "The Proletariat and Nationalism."
Scots Socialist (1946): 4.

   Brown argues that the working classes tend to a
   "narrow nationalism" while the upper classes support
   an internationalism based on money and prestige.
   True nationalism, continues Brown, should be based
   on patterns found in Switzerland, Denmark, Norway and
   other small nations and should encourage an
   internationalism supported by education.

518.   Brown, Oliver. "A Scottish Republicanism?" National
Weekly 4 (Sept. 13, 1952): 3.

   Cautions against the blind acceptance of a republic in
   an independent Scotland.

519.   Brown, Oliver. "The Scottish Socialist Party." Catalyst
(Spring 1969): 20-21.

   Brown recounts the aims of this party, founded on the
   eve of World War II, to oppose the war and Scottish
   participation in it.

520.   Brown, Oliver. "Sham Internationalism." National
Weekly 4 (Jan. 19, 1952): 1.

   Brown points out the differences between imperialism
   and true internationalism.

521.   Byrne, Michael. "First Steps to Self-Government."
Scots Socialist (1948): 3.

   Byrne, a General Secretary of the Scottish Transport
   Union, calls for complete support by the Scottish
   Trade Unions for independence for Scotland in the
   best interests of the Scottish working class.

522.   Burnett, Ray. "Scotland and Antonio Gramsci."
Scottish International 5 (Nov. 1972): 12-15.

   Gramsci, a Sardinian Marxist, has had great influence on
   Scottish left-wing nationalism. Burnett explains why.
   He explains Gramsci's idea of "actualizing" Marxism.

523. Cunningham, Roseanna. "The SNP 79 Group." Crann Tara
(Autumn 1979): 5.

A sketch of the "79 Group" which was formed after the
1979 referendum to promote full independence for
Scotland, with socialist redistribution of power, wealth,
and land under a Scottish Republic.

524. Cunninghame, A.T. "Scottish Nationalism and Imperialism."
The Modern Scot 2 (Summer 1931): 123-127.

In 1931, Cunninghame is shocked at the number of
imperialists within Scottish Nationalist ranks and
reminds them that a free Scotland should never be an
imperialist Scotland.

525. Easton, Norman. "Conceptual Problems for the
Provincial Elect." Crann Tara (Winter 1981): 14-15.

Easton's article addresses British socialists who have
conceptual difficulties with Scottish Nationalism. He
says they should view Scotland as an oppressed colony
and should avoid a false internationalism that preaches
international brotherhood while allowing oppression to
continue in Britain itself. Finally, he condemns them
for blindly following socialist theory without trying
to apply it closer to home.

526. Easton, Norman. "Marxists for Self-Government."
Radical Scotland (Autumn 1982): 16-21.

A case study of the republican faction of the British
Socialist Worker's Party. The SWP was in favor of
devolution in 1977, but apparently against it in 1979,
and Easton accuses them of deliberately avoiding the
issue of an independent socialist Scotland.

527. Garden-Coie, C.G. "Scottish Trade Unionists and
Scottish Nationalism." Scots Independent (June 1949): 7.

Argues for socialism in Scotland alone if Britain as a
whole won't adopt it.

528. Gunn, Neil. "Is the Small Nation Doomed?" Scots
Independent (December 1940): 6.

The famous Scots novelist defends the notion that
small-nation nationalism can result in a truer
internationalism as well.

529. Gunn, Neil. "Literature: Class or National?" Outlook
(July 1936): 54-58.

Gunn argues that Scottish literature can be an expression
of both class and nation and also challenges the view
that nationalism and internationalism are opposed.

530. Hay, George Campbell. "Moab is My Washpot, Edom is My Footstool: Scotland's Irish Analogy." Scots Socialist (March 1941): 4.

> In times of war, England won't be benevolent, so like the Irish in 1916, Scots should "Seize their nationality" and prepare for armed resistance, Hay argues.

531. Hay, George Campbell. "Ours 'Tis to Reason Why." Scots Socialist (September 1940): 4-5.

> Hay, novelist, poet, translator, and Gaelic scholar sees self-government as a means to force Whitehall either to be truly democratic or else cease its rhetoric about British democracy and the rights of nations.

532. Hay, George Campbell. "The Scotland I'd Like to See." New Scot 2 (November 1946): 24-6.

> A war veteran and poet envisions a free Scotland, prosperous and socialist, with a diverse and lively culture liberated from the church and Scottish conservatism and English control.

533. Inverness-shire John MacLean Society. "Nationalism plus Socialism." The Schiltrom 2 (1972): 5-8.

> A defense of a Scottish Socialist Republic.

534. Kerevan, George. "Arguments within Scottish Marxism." Bulletin of Scottish Politics (Spring 1981): 111-133.

> Kerevan analyzes the dilemma of a Scotland rich in Marxist tradition but having relatively few important international Marxists. He also reviews Tony Dickson's Scottish Capitalism (London: Wishart, 1980) and concludes that most Marxist theoreticians of international stature achieve that status when their own nations are achieving some kind of political autonomy.

535. Lamont, Archie. "Is There a Scottish Type of Socialism?" New Alliance 5 (Jan./Feb. 1944): 3-5.

> Lamont contrasts the socialism of small nations, exemplified by Keir Hardie, versus the "Big State" socialism as posited by G.D.H. Cole.

536. Lamont, Archie. "Two Kinds of Nationalism." Scots Independent (January 1933): 42.

> Lamont contrasts the nationalism of aggression and exploitation with small state nationalism resulting in peace and co-operation among small, non-imperialist nations.

537. MacKay, A.B. "Unite Scottish Groups for Self-Government." New Scot 2 (February 1946): 18-19.

A Labour Party member views the Labour Party as the best means to Scottish independence and socialism in Scotland.

538. McKay, Ian. "The Devolution Issue." Scottish Marxist (Spring 1976): 18-23.

McKay says Communists must support an independent Scotland only if it embraces Socialist ideals.

539. MacPherson, Hector. "Imperialism versus Nationalism." Scottish Nation 1 (October 1914): 183-184.

Imperialism doesn't respect another nation's sovereignty while nationalism does so by definition, this article states.

540. McShane, Harry. "John MacLean: a Personal Note." Scots Socialist 53 (1949): 1.

McShane writes of his friendship with MacLean from 1909 onwards, recounting MacLean's role as a teacher and socialist, giving insights into his generosity and integrity, and the effects of his prison sentences.

541. Maxwell, Stephen. "Scotland's Cruel Paradox." Radical Scotland (Feb./March 1983): 12-14.

Summary of Maxwell's argument: Socialists, after years of support, have failed to produce socialism in Scotland and her problems still exist. Socialism is possible in Scotland because of Labour's electoral strength, the weakness of the Tories in Scotland, the collapse of heavy industry and capitalism there, and the future of oil. True socialism will have to come from a more radical base than before, and presupposes Scottish independence.

542. Maxwell, Stephen. "Scottish Radicalism." Question (May 1976): 5-7.

Maxwell finds a distinct Scottish radical tradition in Scots like Keir Hardie, John Grierson, A.D. Lindsay and others.

543. Mitchison, Naomi. "Naomi Mitchison Reviews the Scottish National Party." Scots Independent (October 1945): 1.

Mitchison defends internationalism, condemns mere anti-English racism, and approves the possibility of an independent Scotland which is socialist and internationalist in outlook.

544. Mitchison, Naomi. "Self-Government and the Labour Party." Forum 1 (February 1947): 7-8.

Mitchison explains some Scottish traits and beliefs that English Labour members should consider and understand, particularly the more conservative ideas and the influence of religion, but also the radical and socialist background in Scottish politics.

545. Mitchison, Naomi. "A Socialist Plea for Scotland." Modern Scot 3 (April 1932): 25-30.

Makes distinction between urban and rural socialism and believes rural or "steading" socialism would be more applicable in an independent Scotland.

546. Murray, Alex. "John MacLean 1879-1923: Teacher, Marxist-Nationalist." Scottish Marxist (November 1973): 7-17.

A tribute to John MacLean by a noted Scots Communist.

547. Murray, Alex. "Synopsis of the Communist Party View of the National Question in Scotland." Scottish Marxist (June 1973): 33-43.

A sketch of the support by the Communist Party from the 1930's to the present for a Scottish Parliament in the interests of Scotland's working classes.

548. Murray, Walter. "Nationalism and Internationalism." Scottish Home Rule Association News sheet 4 (September 1923): 17-18.

Small nations having control of their own affairs would make for more international harmony, not less, writes Murray.

549. Nairn, Tom. "Internationalism: A Critique." Bulletin of Scottish Politics (Autumn 1980): 101-125.

Nairn considers the relationship between internationalism and nationalism, and points out the flaws and contradictions in "internationalism". Often, he notes, internationalism is merely a concealed imperialism, lending itself to abuse by large nations and multi-nationals.

550. Orr, Lord Boyd. "World Government and Self Government." Scottish Journal (September 1952): 3.

Orr believes an independent Scotland would bring out the true internationalism for which Scots have long been noted.

551. Purves, Graham. "Calton Hill Break-In." Radical
Scotland (Summer 1982): 12-14.

A complete summary of the Calton Hill Break-In in
October 1981, its historical and legal significance as
well as the complete text of the "Calton Hill Declaration"
which calls for an "independent sovereign Parliament" in
Scotland.

552. Raszkowski, Josef. "Battlepost of the Poor: the Legend
of John MacLean." Cencrastus (Autumn 1979): 9-12.

A thorough commentary on the legendary status of John
MacLean as an "Agitator", as a "Christ figure", as a
"Humanitarian", and his influence on literature, the
screen and stage. Raszkowski sees MacLean as a new hero,
"alongside Bruce and Wallace".

553. Scottish Labour Party. "Scottish Labour Party Policy."
CARN (Autumn 1977): 4-5.

The official policy of the Scottish Labour Party, which
was founded on the 18th of January 1976, giving full
support to an independent socialist Scotland.

554. Scottish Marxist (November 1973)

A special issue devoted to John MacLean 1879-1923.

555. Sillars, Jim. "Why I'm Not in the SNP." Crann Tara
(Winter 1977): 4.

Sillars says the SNP has come to believe that independence
is a goal in itself, while the Scottish Labour Party
believes independence is only the means to a Socialist
Scotland.

556. Smith, A. Clark. "A Study in Confusion." Scots
Socialist 41 (1946): 1.

Smith lists his "seven examples of Scottish confusion
regarding nationalism", including the confusion of
"state" and "nation" and Lenin's problem of centralization
at the expense of nationality in the USSR.

557. Turnbull, Ronald and Beveridge, Craig. "Scottish
Nationalist, British Marxist: the Strange Case of Tom Nairn."
Cencrastus (Summer 1983): 2-5.

A critique and appraisal of Tom Nairn's political thought
and his contributions to Scottish Nationalism.
Investigates Nairn's nationalism and internationalism
and its relation to Marxism; challenges Nairn's evaluation
of Scots culture.

558. Urquhart, James. "Can Scotland Have Home Rule by 1948?" New Scot 2 (March 1947): 2-6.

Socialism, argues Urquhart, is compatible with Scottish Nationalism, and has been supported by the Labour Party since the days of Keir Hardie.

559. Worker's Party of Scotland. "British Road to a Scottish Parliament." Scottish Vanguard 6 (Oct./Nov. 1974): 4-6.

Reconciles Scots self-rule to socialism and concludes that it is necessary for Scotland "to pursue to the utmost the struggle against British imperialism through resolute and self-reliant action.

560. Walkinshaw, Colin. "Socialism: National or International?" Scots Independent (July 1942): 6.

The article observes that nationalist states support war, but that socialist ones do as well. He concludes that small nations, free and prosperous, are more likely to contribute to world peace than are large states.

561. Whitfield, David G. "Antonio Gramsci: Signposts to Scottish Action." Scottish International 6 (Aug. 1973): 6-9.

Whitfield measures the influence of this Sardinian Marxist on Scottish political thought, and explains the relevance of Gramsci's ideas to Scottish Nationalism today.

562. Whyte, J.H. "The Basis of Modern Nationalism." Modern Scot 3 (October 1932): 192-197.

Considers socialism and nationalism and concludes that there are good and bad varieties of both.

563. Wood, Ian S. "John Wheatley: Scottish Labour's Forgotten Man." Radical Scotland (June/July 1983): 23-25.

John Wheatley (1869-1930) was an Irish-born Scottish socialist. Wood summarizes Wheatley's political career. He traces Wheatley's commitment to Home Rule, especially in the 1920's, and tries to guage the influence of Ireland on Wheatley's thinking on Scottish independence.

564. Worker's Party of Scotland. "John MacLean: Proletarian Internationalist-Revolutionary Patriot." Scottish Vanguard 6 (Winter 1973): 6-14.

A thorough summation of MacLean's ideas, on the fiftieth anniversary of MacLean's death. Special attention is paid to MacLean's blend of nationalism and socialism.

565. Worker's Party of Scotland. "Patriotism, Nationalism, Revolution." Scottish Vanguard (Aug./Sept. 1968): 16-18.

A justification for Scottish Nationalism, on the grounds that it will lead to socialism in Scotland and hasten the end of British imperialism.

566. Young, James D. "Socialism and Nationalism in Scotland." Cencrastus (Summer 1982): 32-37.

A sketch of Marxist attitudes to Scottish self-rule before 1917. Young concludes that Scottish Nationalism is not reactionary, but progressive: "An independent Scotland would also create the pre-conditions in which we might just become the first democratic socialist society in Western Europe." Many footnotes and sources given.

7.

HUGH MACDIARMID AND SCOTTISH LIBERATION

He canna Scotland see wha yet canna see the Infinite.
                                    Hugh MacDiarmid
                                    A Drunk Man Looks at the Thistle

Hugh MacDiarmid (1892-1978) was the pseudonym of Christopher
Murray Grieve. MacDiarmid was an awesome blend of many
qualities. He was a unique fusion of communist and nationalist, poet and politician, aristocrat and proletarian, Scot
and world citizen. He was praised by Eliot and Pound, and
is considered by many to be the outstanding poet of the
twentieth century. He did much to revive the Scots language,
and spent much of his time demanding the complete liberation
of the Scottish people, in every facet of collective and
individual life. He was perhaps as great as a polemicist as
he was as a poet, yet much of his prose is overshadowed by
his poetry. The pieces listed here are only representative
of those vast writings. See the sections on the "Language
Question" and "Socialism and Internationalism" for writings
specifically on those topics.

BOOKS BY GRIEVE/MACDIARMID

567. Grieve, C.M. Albyn or Scotland and the Future.
London: Kegan Paul, 1927. 95pp.

   Grieve's recognition of the Scottish Renaissance then
   underway and its effect on every sphere of Scottish life.
   Here appears his famous discussion of "the Caledonian
   antisyzygy" - the blend of opposites, the "diversity in
   unity" of Scottish life and culture.

568. MacDiarmid, Hugh. At the Sign of the Thistle: a
Collection of Essays. London: Nott, 1934. 222pp.

   MacDiarmid on: "The Present Position of the Scottish
   National Movement", "English Ascendancy in British
   Literature", and "The Purpose of a Free Man."

Here, MacDiarmid presents his view of Scottish
Nationalism as a liberating force, freeing the
individual to contribute to a national and
international culture.

569. MacDiarmid, Hugh. The Company I've Kept. London:
Hutchinson, 1966. 288pp.

Autobiographical essays. "John MacLean and the Clydesiders"
and "MacLean's significance today" are portrayals of
MacLean's ideas on an independent socialist Scotland.

570. Grieve, C.M. "Conclusion." In Contemporary Scottish
Studies: First Series. London: Leonard Parsons, 1926,
314-326.

Grieve outlines the means to a Scottish Renaissance,
points to Scotland's educational shortcomings, discusses
Social Credit, and explains why the new Scotland must
undo the work of the Reformation.

571. Grieve, C.M. Contemporary Scottish Studies: First
Series. London: Leonard Parsons, 1926. 344pp.

A series of essays on the state of Scottish culture in
1926. Subjects include drama, art, education, politics,
the best means to a true Scottish national revival,
Douglas Credit, the work of Ruaraidh Erskine, Home Rule,
and others. See especially: "R.E. Muirhead and Scottish
Home Rule".

572. MacDiarmid, Hugh. Cunninghame Graham: a Centenary
Study. Glasgow: Caledonian Press, 1952. 40pp.

An appraisal of Cunninghame Graham's politics, writings,
and individuality.

573. MacDiarmid, Hugh. "English Ascendancy in British
Literature." In At the Sign of the Thistle: A Collection of
Essays. London: Nott, 1934, 11-32.

MacDiarmid writes on the cultural imperialism of England
in Scottish letters and views a bridge between Gaelic
and Scots as one way to combat that imperialism.

574. MacDiarmid, Hugh. Lucky Poet: A Self-Study in Literature
and Political Ideas being the Autobiography of Hugh MacDiarmid.
London: Methuen, 1943. 436pp.

Many of these essays tend to show MacDiarmid's unique
blend of political and cultural nationalism, e.g. "On
seeing Scotland Whole" and "Round the World for Scotland".

575. MacDiarmid, Hugh. A Political Speech. Edinburgh:
Reprographia, 1972. 15pp.

Transcription from a recording taken at a 1320 Club
Symposium at Glasgow University, April 6, 1968.
MacDiarmid argues that Scots are more truly
cosmopolitan than the English. He outlines the major
cultural differences between England and Scotland and
demands complete independence for Scotland in all
realms.

576. MacDiarmid, Hugh. "The Present Position of the
Scottish National Movement." In At the Sign of the Thistle:
a Collection of Essays. London: Nott, 1934, 197-212.

A conception of Scottish Nationalism not merely as a
political force but as an imaginative and creative means
to free the individual Scot from mental and physical
bondage.

577. MacDiarmid, Hugh. "The Purpose of a Free Man." In At
the Sign of the Thistle: a Collection of Essays. London: Nott,
1934, 57-79.

MacDiarmid repeats his defence of Scottish Nationalism
as a liberating force for the individual and as a means
for Scotland to be truly international.

578. Grieve, C.M. "R.E. Muirhead and Scottish Home Rule."
In Contemporary Scottish Studies. London: Leonard Parsons,
1926, 260-267.

A polemic against the Scottish Home Rule Association's
conception of Scottish independence. Grieve sees it as a
party of mediocrity, lacking any creativity or vision.
According to Grieve, Muirhead redeems some of the
Association's bad qualities.

579. Grieve, C.M. "The Hon. Ruaridh Erskine of Mar."
In Contemporary Scottish Studies. London: Leonard Parsons,
1926, 244-250.

An appreciative sketch of the achievements of one of
the great nationalists of the day. Grieve praises
Erskine's work on behalf of Gaelic culture and the
Scottish National League.

580. MacDiarmid, Hugh. "Scotland: Full Circle." In Whither
Scotland? edited by Duncan Glen, 233-250. London: Gollancz,
1971.

Compares the Scotland of 1943 with that of 1970 and
finds things similarly bad.

581. Gibbon, Lewis Grassic, and MacDiarmid, Hugh. _Scottish Scene, or The Intelligent Man's Guide to Albyn_. London: Jarrold's, 1934. 348pp.

> A collection of essays, poems, sketches, stories, plays, newspaper abstracts, etc. Examples of MacDiarmid's ideas on a wide range of political subjects.

582. Grieve, C.M. "Swatches o' Hamespun." In _Contemporary Scottish Studies_. London: Leonard Parsons, 1926, 237-245.

> Essay on the limitations of the Scots language and on its importance to the Scots writer.

ARTICLES BY MACDIARMID, ARRANGED CHRONOLOGICALLY

583. "Scottish Literature and Home Rule." _Scottish Home Rule Association Newsheet_ 3 (November 1922): 26-27.

> MacDiarmid concludes: "Scottish Home Rule and a Scottish Literary Revival of any real consequence presuppose one another.

584. "At the Sign of the Thistle: Programme for a Scottish Fascism." _The Scottish Nation_ (June 19, 1923): 10.

> Advocates an adoption of some variant of fascism to force agrarian reform in Scotland.

585. "Scotland Internationally To-Day." _Scottish Home Rule_ 4 (March 1924): 78.

> Comments on the remarkable interest in Scottish literature shown abroad. Concludes that "the separate spirit of Scotland is a vital and valuable ingredient" of that recognition.

586. "The Future of Scotland." _Scottish Home Rule_ 8 (November 1927): 6.

> Praises G.M. Thomson's work, _Caledonia: or the Future of the Scots_ as an "unanswerable indictment of post-Union policy."

587. "Wider Aspects of Scottish Nationalism." _Scots Independent_ (Nov. 1927): 3-4.

> Advocates Social Credit and a modern nationalism to replace what he terms "sentimental" nationalism.

588. "Scottish Nationalism and the Burns Cult." Pictish
Review 1 (March 1928): 50-51.

A criticism of Scots who adopt Burns for shallow
political and literary aims.

589. "Backward Forward." Pictish Review 1 (May 1928):
74-75.

MacDiarmid criticises the anti-intellectualism of
many Scottish socialists.

590. "Scottish Nationalism and the Local Authorities."
Scots Independent (May 1928): 106-107.

On the importance of having Scottish Nationalists in
local government as a preparation for Scottish
independence at higher levels.

591. "Nationalism and Socialism." Scots Independent
(Sept. 1928): 159-160.

Grieve asks why Scotland can't preserve her national
character the way other nations can. He also urges Scots
to quit pandering to the British political parties.

592. "Scottish Nationalism versus Socialism." Scots
Independent (February 1929): 42-43.

Advocates Social Credit for Scotland, and attacks
Ramsay MacDonald's politics. Concludes that "true
internationalism and true nationalism go hand in hand."

593. "The Imperial and International Relations of Scotland."
Scots Independent (March 1929): 55.

How complete independence for Scotland will halt its
cultural decay.

594. "Towards a Scottish Renaissance: Desirable Lines of
Advance." Scots Independent (May 1929): 89-90.

The Scots Language as a "half-way house to Gaelic; a
plea for the proper teaching of Scots literature and
history. Explains the ultimate goals of nationalism.

595. "Scotland Tomorrow-Fifty Years Hence." Scots
Independent (June 1929): 103-104.

Grieve envisions the Scotland of 1979: Gaelic is the
chief language in a nation freely governed by some
form of fascism. This article is especially valuable
for an understanding of Grieve's views on fascism and
its application in Scotland.

596. "Clan Albainn and Other Matters." <u>Modern Scot</u> 1
(Summer 1930): 7-10.

A defence of the militant group, "Clan Albainn,"
which supported armed resistance in order to achieve
Scottish independence.

597. "Neil Munro and Scottish Nationalism." <u>Scots
Independent</u> (February 1931): 57.

Assessment of the work and ideas of the popular Scots
novelist Neil Munro. Grieve is especially critical of
Munro's indifference to Scotland's political troubles
but he also acknowledges Munro's formidable skills.

598. "Scottish National Development, Civic Publicity,
Tourism, and Other Matters." <u>Modern Scot</u> 2 (Spring 1931):
32-34.

Demand for radical political approach to Scottish
development and a call for more militancy from the
National Party, and praise for the radical politics of
"Clan Albainn."

599. "Social Credit: the Hope of the World." <u>Modern Scot</u> 1
(Winter 1931): 12-19.

An outline of the basic principles of Major C.H. Douglas'
Social Credit theory, which MacDiarmid hopes will
become the social policy of an independent Scotland.

600. "Communism and Nationalism." <u>New Scotland</u> 1 (December
1935): 3.

A letter from Shetland to a Mr. Kerrigan, answering a
charge that nationalism and internationalism are
incompatible. Grieve draws from Marx and Engels to
prove his claim that Scottish Nationalism and communism
are perfectly harmonious.

601. "Scotland, France and Working Class Interests." <u>New
Scotland</u> 1 (October 1935): 1.

A letter stating that in any conflict between England
and France, Scotland should ally with France because
in sympathy with French socialism, Scottish Nationalism
must be "radically proletarian and Republican."

602. "I Want no Empty Unity." <u>New Scotland</u> 1 (March 1936):
1.

The merger of the National Party with the Scottish Party
in 1934 was a mistake, argues MacDiarmid, for he sees it
as a compromise that will soften the radical nature of
Scottish Nationalism.

603. "Constructing the Dynamic Spirit: We Want Life Abundant." New Scotland 1 (May 1936): 3.

   Grieve: "the objective of the Scottish Nationalist Movement is simply and solely to rouse the dynamic spirit of our people."

604. "Scottish Nationalism and the Land Question." Scots Independent (August 1939): 3.

   The importance of radical agrarian reform to an independent Scotland.

605. "William Power and the Regeneration of Scotland." Scots Independent (Sept. 1939): 6.

   A tribute to the journalist and nationalist William Power.

606. "John MacLean, Scotland, and the Communist Party." Scots Socialist (May 1941): 4.

   In praise of John MacLean (1879-1923).

607. "A Scots Communist Looks at Bonnie Prince Charlie." Scots Independent (August 1945): 1.

   A reconciliation of nationalism with communism, declaring the desirability of a "Celtic Soviet Union."

608. "Why Sould Scots Fight Russians?" Scots Independent (May 1946): 2.

   If Scots and English interests are opposed, then the inevitable war with Russia should find the Scots supporting Russia, because of the Russian support of minority cultures. This is one of MacDiarmid's many claims that the Scots would fare better under a Soviet system than under an English one.

609. "What's Wrong with Scottish P.E.N.?" Scots Independent (July 1946): 5.

   MacDiarmid blasts the low state of culture and writing in Scotland.

610. "Reply to Professor's Orr's Contention that "Plastic Scots" has no Future." New Scot 3 (August 1947): 2.

   MacDiarmid's use of a new type Scots language was often called "synthetic" or "plastic" Scots. He replies here that even this "Plastic Scots" serves Scottish poets far better than any form of English could do.

611.   "The Lallans Controversy." Voice of Scotland 4
(June 1948): 41-48.

   Lowland Scots is not merely a language, writes
   MacDiarmid, but the only means for most Scots to avoid
   alienation and psychological damage by expressing
   themseleves at the deepest levels.

612.   "Stalin and the Small Nations." Voice of Scotland 4
(June 1948): 30.

   Contrasts Soviet treatment of minority cultures with the
   British treatment and finds the Soviet treatment
   preferable for Scotland.

613.   "The Whole versus the Part in Scotland: the Need for
an all-in View." National Weekly 1 (Sept. 11, 1948): 8.

   A call for unity and synthesis in Scottish politics
   and culture, resisting the tendency to concentrate on
   petty issues and peripheral concerns. This article is
   one of many by MacDiarmid calling for a broader and
   more philosophical approach to Scottish Nationalism.

614.   "Knoydart Land Seizures." National Weekly 1 (Nov. 28,
1948): 1-2.

   Defends the six men who seized land on the estate of
   Lord Brocket in Knoydart, with the hope that the
   injustice they suffered might spark a national protest.
   MacDiarmid uses this incident to portray the injustice
   of land ownership in Scotland.

615.   "No Belcherising for John MacLean." National Weekly 1
(Dec. 4, 1948): 1-2.

   A tribute to MacLean at a November rally on the 25th
   anniversary of MacLean's death, at a meeting of the
   Scottish-USSR Society.

616.   "The Lessons of the Knoydart Inquiry: Need for
National Action." National Weekly 1 (Jan. 1, 1949): 1.

   A call to action to seize control of Scotland's future
   just as the men seized their lands at Knoydart. This
   article is one of many by MacDiarmid defending the
   Knoydart land seizures.

617.   "Signal to Go Forward." National Weekly 1 (Feb. 12,
1949): 5.

   A report on the Kirriemuir Trial Ballot which resulted
   in 95% support for some form of devolution or Home Rule
   in Scotland. This plebiscite was ignored in the English
   press, which MacDiarmid view here as deliberate.

618. "Scotland and the Export Drive." National Weekly 1 (June 18, 1949): 5.

A review of Arthur Donaldson's Exports: Opportunity or Menace? MacDiarmid agrees with Donaldson that Scotland could function on her own.

619. "The Scottish National Assembly." National Weekly 2 (Nov. 12, 1949): 6.

Why Grieve didn't sign a Covenant, which he didn't think went far enough in its call for a self-governing Scotland.

620. "Is the Heather on Fire at Last?" National Weekly 2 (Dec. 24, 1949): 1-2.

Grieve believes the half million signatures on the Covenant may be the beginning of a powerful force for independence, one that shouldn't be ignored in Westminster and by the major British political parties.

621. "The Coronation Stone." National Weekly 3 (Dec. 31, 1950): 1.

Praise for the daring shown by the takers of the Stone of Scone from Westminster in Dec. 1950. He sees this as a symbol of Scottish resistance and of support for Scottish independence. The Stone was the traditional coronation stone of Scottish kings.

622. "The Scone Stone and other Topics." National Weekly 3 (Jan. 13, 1951): 1.

Several topics: the return of the Stone of Scone to England; diatribe against the Labour Government, and the role and treatment of Scottish conscientious objectors.

623. "The Human Use of Human Beings: the Challenge of Social Crdit." National Weekly 3 (March 10, 1951): 3-4.

Presents the theory of Social Credit.

624. "Scotland's Opportunity Now: Need for Decisive National Action." National Weekly 3 (March 31, 1951): 1.

MacDiarmid dismisses any practical difficulties in Home Rule and advocates decisive, militant action, concluding that "Rights are not granted but taken."

625.   "Dr. MacCormick Fathers an Off-White Mouse."
National Weekly 3 (April 7, 1951): 3.

   Assails MacCormick's suggestion that the Stone of Scone
   spend part of each year in both Scotland and England.
   MacDiarmid sees this as more evidence of Scottish
   mediocrity and cowardice.

626.   "Truth About Stone Sell-Out: How the Reivers Were
Betrayed." National Weekly 3 (April 28, 1951): 1.

   An attack on those responsible for returning the
   Stone of Scone to England.

627.   "Significance of May Day, 1951." National Weekly 3
(May 5, 1951): 4.

   A call for the return to the nationalist tradition of
   Keir Hardie and Bob Smillie, and to their anti-militarism
   and anti-imperialism.

628.   "Cunninghame Graham." National Weekly 3 (June 23, 1951):
3.

   MacDiarmid sees lack of appreciation for Cunninghame
   Graham and a recent neglect by Glasgow University of
   William Power, Scottish Nationalist and journalist,
   as proof of the low level of Scottish culture in 1951.

629.   "Above Politics and Beneath Contempt: the Force of
Nationalism Despite our "Nationalists." National Weekly 4
(Oct. 20, 1951): 1.

   One of MacDiarmid's frequent assaults at what he terms
   the "appalling ineptitude" and philistinism which he
   sees too frequently in the Scottish National Party.
   He argues for a broader conception of Scottish
   Nationalism than the SNP is able or willing to endorse.

630.   "Where Scottish and English Differ." National Weekly 4
(Jan. 19, 1952): 1.

   MacDiarmid explores the major differences between the
   Scots and English expressed in literature and
   architecture.

631.   "The Significance of Cunninghame Graham." National
Weekly 4 (March 15, 1952): 3.

   A tribute to a man whom MacDiarmid calls "this great
   Scotsman."

632. "The Significance of Cunninghame Graham. " <u>National Weekly</u> 4 (March 22, 1952): 3.

A highly sympathetic account and appraisal of Graham's life and work and his contributions to Scottish literature and politics.

633. "English Insolence and Ignorance Again." <u>National Weekly</u> 4 (May 10, 1952): 1.

Analysis of the "anti-Scottish" complex of many Scots, coupled with English racism and prejudice.

634. "The Future of the Scottish Universities." <u>National Weekly</u> 4 (May 31, 1952): 3.

MacDiarmid believes the Scottish Universities are negatively influenced by English practices, especially the practice of boarding students in hostels.

635. "The Future of the Scottish Universities." <u>National Weekly</u> 4 (June 7, 1952): 2.

MacDiarmid attacks a trend he sees toward Anglicization of the Scottish universities.

636. "The Significance of John MacLean." <u>National Weekly</u> 4 (June 14, 1952): 1.

Explains MacLean's unique nationalism while remaining, in MacDiarmid's words, "an outstanding fighter for Revolutionary Socialism."

637. "The Significance of John MacLean." <u>National Weekly</u> 4 (June 28, 1952): 3.

Comments on the neglect of John MacLean in Scotland and why that neglect should end.

638. "The Significance of John MacLean." <u>National Weekly</u> 4 (July 5, 1952): 4.

Concludes his series on MacLean and dismisses the notion of MacLean's alleged mental illness. He views MacLean's life and work as having fresh significance in Scotland's future.

639. "A Brief Survey of Scottish Politics." <u>National Weekly</u> 5 (Oct. 4, 1952): 2.

The effects of English imperialism and religion. The need for separate political action by Scotland's working class, and the now urgent necessity for Scottish Home Rule.

640. "The Late Mr. C.H. Douglas." National Weekly 5
(Oct. 11, 1952): 1.

Valedictory tribute to Douglas who died in Perth on the
29th of September, 1952, and whose Social Credit theories
had great influence on MacDiarmid.

641. "The Late Mr. Douglas." National Weekly 5 (Oct. 25,
1952): 2.

An analysis of Douglas' theory of "Money Monopoly."

642. "The Late Mr. C.H. Douglas III." National Weekly 5
(Nov. 8, 1952): 3.

MacDiarmid's acknowledgement of his debts to Douglas,
whom he calls a "great Scotsman." Douglas' theory of
Social Credit had great impact on MacDiarmid, Ezra
Pound, and other poets and intellectuals of the 1930's.
Douglas' ideas were tried with some success in Canada.

643. "Economic Independence for the Individual." Scottish
Journal (Christmas 1952): 4-5.

A tribute to Clifford Hugh Douglas who died in Perth
on Sept. 29, 1952, aged 73. MacDiarmid praises Douglas'
"social credit" theories which were tried with some
success in Alberta and British Columbia. He terms
social credit as "Scottish Nationalism's Great Lost
Chance" and as a system "designed to bring about the
economic independence and complete freedom of the
individual."

644. "To Hell with Culture: the Real versus the Pseudo."
National Weekly 5 (May 23, 1953): 3.

MacDiarmid restates his well-known view that culture
is a matter of great importance to Scottish liberation
and is not merely a matter of museums, libraries, and
university degrees.

645. "The Close Brethren of the SNP Junta." Sgian Dubh 5
(Feb. 1968):7-9.

A scathing attack on the Scottish National Party
leadership for its "mediocrity" and narrow vision.

646. "A Sticking Plaster for a Fractured Skull." Catalyst
(Summer 1968): 22-23.

A review of Paton's The Claim of Scotland. He argues
against Paton's belief that the English will listen to
reasoned argument. By contrast, MacDiarmid urges
Scottish resistance by any means necessary to avoid
genocide, and should channel traditional Scottish
violence into political activity.

647. "On Sgian Dubh: Fifth Birthday." Sgian Dubh 5
(Sept. 1968): 3-4.

MacDiarmid praises the magazine Sgian Dubh on its
fifth birthday for its "integrity, industry, and
intellectual acumen."

648. "Separating the Sheep from the Goats: Our National
Heritage Versus a Mess of Pottage." Catalyst (Autumn 1969):
15-17.

A review of Harry Hanham's Scottish Nationalism.
MacDiarmid also criticizes the SNP for its
policies.

649. "A Message from Hugh MacDiarmid." Sgian Dubh 10
(Sept. 1973): 3-4.

A tribute to Sgian Dubh for its provocative stand, with
special praise for F.A.C. Boothby's editorship.

BOOKS ABOUT MACDIARMID

650. Ascherson, Neal. "MacDiarmid and Politics." In The Age
of MacDiarmid, edited by P.H. Scott and A.C. Davies, 224-
237. Edinburgh: Mainstream, 1980.

Interesting discussion on the vagaries of MacDiarmid's
politics, including his little-known ideas on fascism,
his racism and Anglophobia, his unusual lack of interest
in the Spanish Civil War, and the conflict between
his communism and his nationalism.

651. Buthlay, Kenneth. Hugh MacDiarmid. Edinburgh: Oliver
and Boyd, 1964. 125pp.

An important biography on MacDiarmid; includes a select
bibliography of his verse and translations,with
information on his editorial prose and other non-
literary work.

652. Duval, K.D., and Smith, Sydney Goodsir. Hugh MacDiarmid:
a Festschrift. Edinburgh: K.D. Duval, 1962. 221pp. bibl.

A tribute to MacDiarmid by many of Scotland's leading
writers: Smith, Edwin Morgan, Maurice Lindsay, and
Douglas Young. Young's "The Nationalism of Hugh
MacDiarmid," stresses MacDiarmid's immense contribution
to Scottish nationality through his poetry alone.

653.   Glen, Duncan, ed. Hugh MacDiarmid: A Critical Survey.
Edinburgh: Scottish Academic Press, 1972. 241pp. bibl.

Glen's purpose was to make available the best essays on
MacDiarmid's life and work. Most of the contributors are
well-known in their own right: David Daiches, Burns
Singer, Iain Crichton Smith, Tom Scott, and Edwin Morgan.

654.   Glen, Duncan. Hugh MacDiarmid and the Scottish
Renaissance. Edinburgh: Chambers, 1964. 294pp. bibl.

All facets of MacDiarmid's life, work, and influence are
presented. His poetry, politics, philosophy, and feuds
are studied in light of tradition and of the influences
on Scotland's current generation of writers.

655.   Glen, Duncan, ed. Selected Essays of Hugh MacDiarmid.
London: Jonathan Cape, 1969. 252pp.

A selection of MacDiarmid's prose writings, not
previously collected in book form. These may be of
special interest to students of Scottish Nationalism:
"The Quality of Scots Internationalism"; "Towards a
Celtic Front"; Contemporary Scottish Literature and the
National Question"; and "The Upsurge of Scottish
Nationalism".

656.   Maxwell, Stephen. "The Nationalism of Hugh MacDiarmid."
In The Age of MacDiarmid, edited by P.H. Scott and A.C.
Davies, 202-223. Edinburgh: Mainstream, 1980.

Maxwell relates MacDiarmid's nationalism as a changing,
highly complex affair, more potential than actual, and
sees it being influenced heavily by John MacLean, but
also by the Norwegian folklorists of the late 19th
century.

657.   Murison, David."The Language Problem in Hugh Mac-
Diarmid's Work." In The Age of MacDiarmid, edited by P.H.
Scott and A.C. Davies, 83-99. Edinburgh: Mainstream, 1980.

Scots and "synthetic Scots"; influences on MacDiarmid's
Scots poetry; detailed presentation of MacDiarmid's
theories on language and on the meaning of the Scots
language to the individual Scot.

658.   Scott, P.H., and Davies, A.C. The Age of MacDiarmid:
Essays on Hugh MacDiarmid and His Influence on Contemporary
Scotland. Edinburgh: Mainstream, 1980. 268pp.

Many of Scotland's leading scholars and writers pay
tribute to MacDiarmid. They touch on MacDiarmid's
politics, nationalism and communism, his influence on
language and literature, and his international
significance.

659.   Wright, Gordon. MacDiarmid: an Illustrated Biography.
Edinburgh: G. Wright Publishing, 1977. 176pp.

Text, with excellent photographs. Many photos of
MacDiarmid and leading Scottish Nationalists. A
chronology and checklist of publications.

660.   Young, Douglas. "The Nationalism of Hugh MacDiarmid."
In Hugh MacDiarmid: a Festschrift, edited by S.G. Smith and
K.D. Duval, 101-113. Edinburgh: Duval, 1962.

The literary and political aspects of MacDiarmid's
nationalism, which, concludes Young, gave Scotland a
"renewed awareness of Scottish nationality."

ARTICLES ABOUT MACDIARMID

661.   Leslie, Arthur. "The Politics and Poetry of Hugh
MacDiarmid." National Weekly 4 (July 18, 1952): 1.

MacDiarmid's radical republicanism and its reflection in
his early verse.

662.   Leslie, Arthur. "The Politics and Poetry of Hugh
MacDiarmid." National Weekly 4 (July 26, 1952): 3-4.

Short article on MacDiarmid's unorthodox communism.

663.   Leslie, Arthur. "The Politics and Poetry of Hugh
MacDiarmid." National Weekly 4 (Aug. 2, 1952): 3.

Reconciles MacDiarmid's apparent elitism with his
genuine concern for the Scottish working class.

664.   Leslie, Arthur. "The Politics and Peotry of Hugh
MacDiarmid." National Weekly 4 (Aug. 16, 1952): 4.

Concludes the series with a consideration of MacDiarmid's
best later poetry and the political influences on it.

665.   Ross, Raymond J. "Hugh MacDiarmid and John MacLean."
Cencrastus no. 11 (1983): 33-36.

Examines the influence of MacLean on MacDiarmid and the
mythical aspects of MacLean's life and character as
interpreted by MacDiarmid.

8.

THE LANGUAGE QUESTION

I first became interested in Scottish Nationalism when my
mother told me how, as a schoolgirl, she was forced to wear
a wooden board around her neck for not learning English fast
enough.

> John MacCormick
> Co-founder, Scottish National
> Party

Language revival has often been at the vital center of most
national movements. Israel and Ireland are two very good
examples. However, in Scotland the relationship between
language and Scottish Nationalism has not always been
strong or clear. Gaelic, Scotland's oldest language, was
once spoken everywhere in Scotland, while Lowland Scots
has a long and distinguished literary history going back
to the courts of the Middle Ages. Today, Gaelic is spoken
by perhaps 80,000 to 90,000 persons, while Scots is
actively discouraged in the home and schools. Not all
language revivalists are nationalists, and certainly, not
all nationalists place a high priority on Scotland's
languages and their survival. However, Scottish Nationalists
like Ruaridh Erskine and Hugh MacDiarmid believed language
revival was the raison d'etre of political nationalism.
Today, the Scottish National Party has given Gaelic official
language status, and Lowland Scots is given more official
encouragement than it has had in the past. It now seems fair
to say that nobody can truly understand Scottish Nationalism
without some understanding of Scotland's "Language Question."
Even most people who don't rate language revival as a top
priority in Scotland would admit that an independent
Scottish government would do more to prevent cultural decline
than any London-based government would care to do. Meanwhile,
many concerned individuals and organizations are doing their
utmost to prevent the death of Gaelic and Scots, a death
many see as undesirable but inevitable.

BOTH GAELIC AND SCOTS

666. Aitken, A.J. and MacArthur, Tom. Languages of
Scotland. Edinburgh: Chambers, 1979. 160pp.

A thorough consideration of the teaching and promotion
of both Scots and Gaelic in Scottish life. They urge
the teaching of these languages at all levels, both
formally and informally, stating that government
support is absolutely essential. However, both writers
also stress that language must be "living" and not
merely something given academic and official support.

667. Cairns, Robert. "The Languages of Scotland." Scotia
Review (April 1974): 20-26.

A review of Scotland's many languages in historical
times. Cairns notes that Scotland has always been
multi-lingual and should not promote Scots, Gaelic, or
English at the expense of each other.

668. Easton, Norman. "The People's Tongue: Socialist
Thoughts on Scotland's Language." Radical Scotland (Summer
1982): 16-20.

Easton writes on the relationship between class and
language, and concludes that nationalists and socialists
should consider attacks on languages as attacks on the
people who speak them, especially since Gaelic and Scots
are used most widely in working class Scotland.

669. Ellis, P.B. "Introduction." In The Problem of Language
Revival. Inverness: Club Leabhar, 1971, 5-9.

Ellis emphasizes the political and cultural importance
of language survival and shows how "language, thought
and culture are inseparable."

670. Ellis, P.B. "The Problem of Language Revival." In
The Problem of Language Revival. Inverness: Club Leabhar,
1971, 142-146.

Scotland is the worst country for language revival,
argues Ellis because of its hostility to Gaelic.
Ellis considers Israel a successful example of language
revival and advises other nations to study her methods
carefully.

671. Gramsci, Antonio. "A Letter." (translated by Hamish
Henderson). Calgacus 2 (Summer 1975): 3.

Letter from Gramsci to his sister stressing the value
of Sardinian and of bilingualism. Gramsci's writings
have had tremendous influence on Scottish Nationalists.
Gramsci was in prison in Milan at the time of the letter.

672. Heusaff, Alan. "Bulwarks of Political Freedom." In
The Annual Book of the Celtic League, 17-28. Dublin: The
Celtic League, 1966.

    Heusaff demonstrates how language revival is a prelude
    to political pride and resistance.

673. Lewis, E. Glyn. Bilingualism and Bilingual Education.
Oxford: Pergamon Press, 1981. 455pp.

    A definitive work on bilingualism. Discusses theories
    of bilingualism, with case studies from America, the
    Soviet Union, and the Celtic regions. The needs and
    policies of bilingual education. Scotland is discussed
    in some detail. Strong emphasis on the Welsh experience.
    Encyclopedic in its detail. Excellent and lengthy
    select bibliography on bilingualism throughout the
    world.

674. MacGregor, Forbes. "Languages of Scotland." Scotia
Review (December 1972): 13-17.

    General view of both Scots and Gaelic as part of
    Scotland's linguistic heritage.

675. Neill, William. "The Despised Heritage." Catalyst
(December 1967): 3-4.

    Argues for Scots and Gaelic bilingualism throughout
    Scotland.

676. Neill, William. "Language and Scotland." Catalyst
(Spring 1970): 10-11.

    Neill believes in equal status for Scots and Gaelic and
    argues that either language should be used as a
    medium in government and education.

677. Mitchison, Naomi. "Gaelic With an Oxford Accent."
Scots Independent (March 1942): 2.

    A call for the education authorities to do more to
    promote Scots and Gaelic, by a leading novelist and
    socialist.

678. Quirk, Randolph. "Language and Nationhood." In The
Crown and the Thistle, edited by Colin MacLean, 56-69.
Edinburgh: Scottish Academic Press, 1979.

    How language is often without political boundary.
    Discusses nations without languages and languages
    without nations.

679.   Turnbull, Ronald, and Beveridge, Craig. "The Myth of Scottish Inarticulacy." Bulletin of Scottish Politics, (Spring 1982): 134-138.

   The authors challenge the view that Scots are unable to communicate properly because of political and cultural oppression and sense of linguistic inferiority.

680.   Williams, J.C. "Bilingualism Today." In Celtic League Annual, 4-16. Dublin: The Celtic League, 1967.

   Programs for teaching bilingualism in the Celtic nations without sacrificing the native language.

681.   Wood, Richard E. "Scotland: the Unfinished Quest for Linguistic Identity." Word 30 (1979): 186-202.

   An introduction to the problems confronting Gaelic, Broad Scots, and English in Scotland. Wood clarifies the relationship between politics, nationalism, and language revival or survival. The article includes a useful list of agencies concerned with Scotland's languages. An excellent general overview looking into the language question in Scotland.

GAELIC

Books and Pamphlets

682.   Campbell, John Lorne. Gaelic in Scottish Education and Life. Edinburgh: Johnston, 1945. 106pp. bibl.

   One of the standard works on Gaelic. Chapters and topics include: "Gaelic in Scottish Life," "Gaelic in Scottish Education," "Bilingualism in the Empire and Abroad," and "Restoration of Scottish Gaelic." His areas of concern: schools, broadcasting, place names, and many more.

683.   Dorian, Nancy C. Language Death: the Life Cycle of a Scottish Gaelic Dialect. Philadelphia: U. of Penn. Press, 1981. 206pp. bibl.

   A thorough study of Gaelic in East Sutherland over a period of 16 years. Scholarly. Themes: bilingualism, language death and suicide, language loyalty, government assistance. Lengthy bibliography of Gaelic and related studies.

684. MacAoidh, Domhnall. "Scotland and Gaelic." In Celtic
League Annual, 53-58. Dublin: The Celtic League, 1967.

A review of An Comunn Gaidhealach (The Gaelic League),
since its founding in 1891 to promote Gaelic. The
author of this article feels the government is not
giving enough official support to Gaelic.

685. MacDonald, Martin. "The Media." In Gaelic in Scotland,
edited by Derick Thomson, 57-65. Glasgow: Gairm, 1976.

What the media can do to promote Gaelic language and
culture.

686. Mackay, D.J. "Nationality and Culture." In The Celtic
League Annual, 31-34. Dublin: The Celtic League, 1968.

What Gaelic can contribute to Scotland as a whole.

687. MacKay, I.R. Gaelic Is... Inverness: An Comunn
Gaidhealach, 1969, 6pp.

A pamphlet in a series put out by the Gaelic League to
promote Gaelic and Highland culture. This pamphlet gives
historical instances of oppression of Gaelic, and the
work done by An Comunn Gaidhealach to overcome that
oppression. MacKay compares Gaelic unfavorably with the
status of languages in other countries, including the
Soviet Union. He believes that Gaelic has great practical
value and should be encouraged as a living language and
not just as a literary one.

688. MacKinnon, Kenneth. Language, Education and Social
Processes in a Gaelic Community. London: Routledge, 1977.
222pp.

Another important work on Gaelic. Mackinnon studies the
problems of Gaelic and bilingualism from a sociologist's
point of view. Bilingual education requires specially
trained teachers and suitable learning aids and texts.
Both he finds lacking in most Gaelic schools. Social
attitudes of the Gaels themselves make language learning
difficult. Mackinnon sees hope for Gaelic despite
the low morale in the Gaelic areas at present.

689. MacKinnon, Kenneth. Language Shift and Education:
Conservation of Ethnolinguistic Culture amongst School-
children in a Gaelic Community. London: Hatfield Polytechnic,
1977. 25pp.

A study on pupils in Harris, 1972-1974. Mackinnon found
that most children had a positive view of Gaelic
and he concludes that the schools could be doing a lot
more than they are to encourage and cultivate those
positive views.

690. Mackinnon, Kenneth. The Lion's Tongue. Inverness: Club Leabhar, 1974. 132pp.

A standard general work on the history and future of Scottish Gaelic. Mackinnon considers the language in its social setting and recommends new approaches in teaching. He suggests careful selection of study materials. The government can do far more, he states.

691. MacLennan, Gordon. "New Hope for Gaelic." In The Annual Book of the Celtic League, 68-73. Dublin: The Celtic League, 1966.

Comments on the significance of the appointment in 1965 of a full-time director to run An Comunn Gaidhealach, and how the policy of this organization has become more outspoken and militant in defense of Gaelic.

692. MacLeod, Donald J. "Gaelic in Public Life." In Gaelic in Scotland, edited by Derick Thomson, 24-27.

MacLeod lists the prerequisites for public use of Gaelic: community education, a halt to emigration from the Highlands, unity of all agencies concerned with Gaelic, and the political good will and protection of politicians, especially those belonging to Scottish Nationalist parties.

693. Murray, Duncan C. "The Languages of Scotland." In The Celtic League Annual, 36-41. Dublin: The Celtic League,

Historical sketch of Scotland's many languages up to the time of the Scottish National Party's recognition of Gaelic as an official language of Scotland.

694. Thomson, Derick., ed. Gaelic in Scotland. Glasgow: Gairm, 1976. 92pp.

Several contributors make recommendations for the health of Gaelic in public life, in the shops, in the schools, in the government, and in the media. A thorough discussion of the problems and solutions of Gaelic language use in Scotland. Thomson is one of the foremost poets in Gaelic in Scotland today.

695. Thomson, Derick. "Gaelic in Scotland." In Gaelic in Scotland, edited by Derick Thomson, 1-10. Glasgow: Gairm, 1976.

A brief history of Gaelic by a leading Gaelic poet.

696. Stephens, Meic. "The Gaels of Scotland." In Linguistic Minorities in Western Europe. Llandysul: Gomer, 1976, 51-77.

An historic account of the Gaelic language in Scotland, its persecution and revival, and future prospects.

GAELIC

Articles

697. Brown, Oliver. "Gaelic and Politics." Scots
Independent (November 1934): 201.

> Brown thinks Gaelic language is vital to the economic
> life of the Highlands and thus deserves government
> protection.

698. Donn, Thomas MacKenzie. "The Debate About the Gaelic
Language of Scotland Since 1832." Transactions of the Gaelic
Society of Inverness 49 (Dec. 1974): 26-52.

> Powerful arguments for the study and preservation of
> Gaelic.

699. Mar, Earl of. "Gaelic Manifesto." Fiery Cross (April
1907): 5.

> Support for the teaching of Gaelic in all schools in
> Scotland. Government officials should also be required
> to speak, read, and write Gaelic, he argues.

700. Hamilton, James. "A Forgotten Heritage." CARN (Autumn
1976): 2-3.

> Hamilton asks why Scottish Nationalists haven't stressed
> language more, and attacks the belief that Gaelic has
> no relevance to the Lowlands and to urban Scotland,
> noting that Gaelic or Celtic place names outnumber all
> others in Scotland by 10-1.

701. Hay, George Campbell. "Gael Warning." Scots Review 8
(November 1947): 104-105.

> A Gaelic poet and translator issues a militant call
> to resist the extermination of Gaelic.

702. Lloyd, Ifan. "The Lowland Myth of Scotland-Part One."
CARN (Autumn 1978): 3-4.

> Lloyd shows the extent of the Gaelic heritage in Lowland
> Scotland.

703. Lloyd, Ifan. "The Lowland Myth in Scotland-Part Two."
CARN (Winter 1978): 3-5.

> Lloyd challenges the myth that Gaelic disappeared from
> the Scottish Lowlands in 1100. Instead, he gives figures
> to indicate that as many as 45% of Scots spoke Gaelic
> as late as 1500, and 1 in 4 as late as 1600, including
> a high percentage of Lowlanders.

704. MacDonald, Neil. "The Worth of Gaelic." <u>National Weekly</u> 5 (Dec. 6, 1952): 2.

A defense of Gaelic culture and language, with emphasis on its practical value in the Highlands.

705. MacKinnon, Kenneth. "A Gaelic Revival." <u>New Society</u> (March 11, 1976): 562-563.

Although Gaelic receives little support from political parties, including the Scottish National Party, the 1971 census showed a 10.5% increase in the number of Gaelic bilinguals, very encouraging to Mackinnon.

706. Mackinnon, Kenneth. "Gaelic's Rearguard Fight." <u>Scots Independent</u> (December 1943): 7.

Gaelic has been victimized by racial prejudice says Mackinnon, and only a national government can properly protect and promote the language. Mackinnon does not believe that Gaelic is doomed.

707. Mackinnon, Kenneth. "The School in Gaelic Scotland." <u>Transactions of the Gaelic Society of Inverness</u> 47 (1971-72): 374-389.

Historical account of Gaelic, with suggestions for the future, quoting the 1951 UNESCO REPORT on "The Use of Vernacular Languages in Education," supporting bilingualism. Mackinnon recommends linking Gaelic to regional planning, ecology, sociology, and other practical endeavors.

708. MacLaren, Duncan. "Civil Rights." <u>Crann Tara</u> (Summer 1978): 13.

MacLaren urges the SNP to guarantee the rights of Gaelic speakers to speak, read, and write anywhere in Scotland in their own language.

709. MacLaren, Duncan. "Good Signs for Gaelic." <u>Question</u> (October 1976): 5.

Discusses <u>Gaelic in Scotland</u> and endorses the proposed Commission on Gaelic for Scotland.

710. Maclean, Sorley. "Problems of Gaelic Education." <u>Catalyst</u> (Autumn 1969): 21-22.

Maclean examines the problems of teaching and learning Gaelic and proposes solutions to those problems.

711. Maclean, Sorley. "Problems of Gaelic Education."
Catalyst (Winter 1970): 9-10.

The noted Gaelic poet suggests a way in which Gaelic can
achieve prominence in Scotland.

712. Mulholland, Robert. "Scotland's Future: Ends Before
Means." Scotia Review (August 1972): 16-19.

Gaelic must be given special attention and status in a
socialist Scotland, argues Mulholland.

713. Mulholland, Robert. "Scottish Concepts in Language,
Literature, and Nationality." Scotia Review (December 1973):
49-55.

The only way Scotland can reverse the trend to English
cultural dominance is to adopt Scotland's Gaelic
Language as its official language, argues Mulholland.
In defense, he quotes MacDiarmid: "A Scottish Scotland
must be a Gaelic Scotland." (MacDiarmid's The Lucky Poet.)

714. MacThomais, Frang. "On the Gaelic Front." CARN (Winter
1983): 3.

In 1971, there were 81,000 speakers of Gaelic in
Scotland, while the 1981 census reveals 79,000.
However, the author of the article notes an increase in
the number of people able to read and write Gaelic,
especially in the Lowlands. A strong united front will
be necessary to preserve the language into the 21st
century.

715. Thompson, Frank. "Gaelic: Its Death in our Time?"
Scotia Review (August 1973): 12-15.

Thompson believes the key to any language survival
rests with the number of monoglot speakers. There were
28,000 in 1900 and only 974 in 1961. He calls for
emergency measures to rescue Gaelic.

716. Thompson, F.G. "Gaelic in Politics. " Transactions of
the Gaelic Society of Inverness. 47 (1971-72): 67-100.

Traces the role of Gaelic's influence in many of Scotland's
leading political movements such as the Highland Land
League and the Home Rule Association.

THE SCOTS LANGUAGE (BROAD SCOTS, LALLANS)

Books and Pamphlets

717.   Daiches, David. Literature and Gentility in Scotland.
Edinburgh: Edinburgh University Press, 1982. 114pp.

A noted scholar traces the history of the Scots
language in literature and explains MacDiarmid's
attempts to revive and expand Scots. Daiches
evaluates MacDiarmid's contributions and efforts.

718.   McClure, J. Derrick., Aitken, A.J., and Low, John
Thomas. The Scots Language: Planning for Modern Usage.
Edinburgh: Ramsay Head Press, 1980. 95pp.

A comprehensive view of the future of Scots in
education, literature, society, and the home. Practical
methods are suggested not only to preserve the
language but to develop its further use.

719.   Mackie, Albert. "Hugh MacDiarmid and the Scottish
Language." In Hugh MacDiarmid: a Festschrift, edited by
K.D. Duval, 165-185. Edinburgh: Duval, 1962.

Discussion of the history of Scots, Middle Scots, and of
MacDiarmid's successes and failures in his use of Scots
and of his attempts to apply Scots to more universal
themes.

720.   Stephens, Meic. "The Lowland Scots." In Linguistic
Minorities in Western Europe. Llandysul: Gomer, 1976, 78-102.

A historical account of the Scots language and its
struggles to maintain itself as a separate language and
not a mere dialect; its revival and future prospects,
and its relationship with politics and Scottish Nationalism.

THE SCOTS LANGUAGE (BROAD SCOTS, LALLANS)

Articles

721.   Bold, Alan. "Why I Chose English." Chapman (November
1970):3.

A modern Scots poet discusses his choice of English
over Scots.

722. Borrowman, Lorna S. "Scots in Education." Chapman
(Spring 1979): 51-54.

    A call for the Scottish education system to foster the
    Scots language at all levels, with several successful
    examples of this being done.

723. Garioch, Robert. "The Use of Scots." Scottish
International (Jan. 1968): 33-35.

    Garioch, a successful poet in Scots, defends the creative
    use of Scots as an adaptable language, good for all
    styles and forms.

724. Glen, Duncan. "Scotland and the Scots." Catalyst
(Winter, 1970): 3-5.

    As a poet, Glen presents the problems facing writers in
    Scots, notably publishing facilities and a limited
    audience, yet the only alternative would be to write in
    a sterile English.

725. Henderson, Thomas. "Scots in the School." Scots
Independent (May 1932): 105.

    A plea for the study of Scots poetry and prose, and the
    need for graded texts, especially for children.

726. Keys, David R. "On the Scottish Language and its
Influence on English." The Scottish Patriot (Dec. 1905):
344-345.

    Traces separate development of Scots and its affinity
    with German and its absorption of French and Norman,
    and its huge influence on English.

727. Lamont, Archie. "Scots Tongue in Northern Ireland."
National Weekly 5 (Oct. 18, 1952): 3.

    The survival and use of Scots in Northern Ireland.

728. Low, John. "English for the Scots." Books in Scotland
(Winter 1981-82): 4-5.

    A strong criticism of the state of education in the
    Scots language in the schools of Scotland.

729. Low, John T. "Writing Scots Prose Today." Books in
Scotland (Winter 1978-79): 9-10.

    Low admits that Scots has always had a place in poetry,
    but its prose use should become more than a matter of
    dictionaries and word books, by becoming a true vehicle
    of creativity for those who speak and write it.

730. McClure, J. Derick. "The Concept of Standard Scots."
Chapman (Spring 1979): 90-99.

   The difficulties in arriving at a much-needed form of
   standard Scots.

731. MacDiarmid, M.P. "Scottish Studies Today: a Comment."
Chapman (Spring 1979): 23-24.

   MacDiarmid asks why so much attention has been given to
   Scots language and literature by international scholars
   when most Scots remain unaware of the richness of Scots
   language.

732. MacDougal, Roderick. "Has Scots a Future?" Scots Review
11 (October 1950): 126.

   National independence without preserving the Scots
   language would be a national disgrace, states MacDougal.
   He believes the revival of the Scots language should be
   a major goal of an independent Scotland.

733. MacGillivray, Alan. "Scots in the Colleges of Education."
Chapman (Spring 1979): 55-57.

   The good work that is being done in Scottish colleges of
   education with regard to graded texts and other Scots
   language aids.

734. Mackie, Albert D. "Written Scots and Spoken Scots."
Books in Scotland (Autumn 1979): 8-9.

   Mackie's recommendations for the Scots language.

735. Muir, Edwin. "A Literature Without a Language."
Outlook (June 1936): 84-89.

   A famous Scottish poet observes that an individual needs
   a language that can express his total nature - both
   sentiment and thought. Often, Scots has expressed one
   part of a Scotsman's personality and English another,
   with disastrous effects to the psyche and to the nation's
   culture, argues Muir.

736. Murison, David. "The Future of Scots." Chapman (Spring
1979): 58-62.

   Murison, a leading expert on the Scots language, believes
   that education will not take the place of Scots used in
   the street and in the home, and that only an independent
   Scotland could insure its survival.

737. Murison, David. "We Can Save the Scots Tongue." <u>New Scot</u> 3 (Sept. 1947): 16-17.

Murison, editor of the <u>Scottish National Dictionary</u>, compares Scotland's need to standardize Scots with Norway's similar problems in arriving at "New Norse" as a compromise: hard work, but necessary, he believes, in promoting Scots.

738. Scott, Tom. "Chairs of Scottish Literature in Scottish Universities." <u>Catalyst</u> (Autumn 1968): 16-17.

No chairs of Scottish literature existed at the time of this article, and Scott, a poet, finds irony that most of the good writers and scholars in Scots must work abroad.

739. Smith, Sydney Goodsir. "In Defence of Lallans." <u>Scots Review</u> 9 (May 1948).

A leading Scots language poet finds Scots neither dead, archaic, nor artificial, speaking eloquently on its potential and diversity in letters and in everyday use.

740. Young, Douglas. "Reply to Professor John Orr." <u>New Scot</u> 3 (August 1947): 11.

Counters the view that Scots has no future by citing examples of successful language nurture in Norway, South Africa, and Belgium.

9.

MODELS FOR SMALL
NATIONS: SCOTTISH
OPTIONS

Small states, in the interest of the common good, cannot be
denied their right to political freedom.
                                        Pope John XXIII
                                        "Pacem in Terris," Encyclical

Skepticism and practicality are seen by outsiders as fairly
typical features of the Scottish character, and Scottish
Nationalists are often required by other Scots to prove
with statistics (or, by example) how independence can be
achieved and maintained by the poorer or smaller regions of
Britain. Scottish Nationalists have thus been very diligent
in their attempts to find models and paradigms for the
political success of small nations. Many nations have been
chosen as paradigms for Scotland to copy, including Ireland,
Israel, Norway, Switzerland, and Denmark. Nationalists in
Scotland are still being required to prove by example and
by parallel, so the search for a model will probably continue.
Meanwhile, the search for models also asks how independent
small nations will in turn treat their own regions and
minorities. In Scotland, the Orkney and Shetland Islands,
long more Norse than Scottish, are demanding answers and
models of their own. The "Orkney and Shetland Question"
thus becomes part of that search for independence and
democracy.

BOOKS AND PAMPHLETS

741. Ellis, P. Beresford. The Problem of Language Revival.
Inverness: Club Leabhar, 1971. 147pp.

    Ellis lists 20 successful modern instances of language
    revival, including examples from Albania, Armenia,
    Denmark, England, and the Faroes. Ellis believes that
    Scotland's own attitudes to language and nationality
    are the worst in Celtic Europe. Ellis argues that
    language revival in most cases is inseparable from
    political survival.

742. Esman, Milton J., ed. Ethnic Conflict in the Western
World. Ithaca: Cornell, 1977. 399pp.

    Historical and theoretical case studies: Belgium, the
    Basques, Quebec, Yugoslavia. The section, "Scottish
    Nationalism, North Sea Oil and the British Response,"
    accounts for the many complex factors which gave rise
    to Scottish political success in the 1970's.

743. Heusaff, Alan. "Bilingualism in Practice." In Celtic
League Annual, 17-29. Dublin: The Celtic League, 1967.

    Examples of bilingualism from Friesland, Switzerland,
    Sweden, Italy, Spain, and other European nations.
    The political nature of bilingualism is examined.
    Heusaff cautions that bilingualism still tends to
    result in dominant languages, and that the true key to
    language survival rests with a large monoglot community.

744. Lamont, Archie. Small Nations. Glasgow: Maclellan,
1944. 160pp.

    Using Denmark, Finland, Sweden, and other small nations
    as examples, Lamont notes that true internationalism
    depends on the freedom of small non-agressor states.
    Scotland could become one of these successful small
    states, concludes Lamont.

745. Naert, Pierre. "Language and Culture." In Book of the
Celtic League, 89-94. Cardiff: The Celtic League, 1965.

    Examples of successful bilingualism in Sweden and Finland,
    concludes that language revival has a strong political
    element in it.

746. O'Conchuir, Padraig. "Celtic Speaking National
Assemblies." In Celtic League Annual, edited by Frank
Thompson, 28-49. Dublin: The Celtic League, 1970.

    Why Scotland should adopt a federal system similar to
    Switzerland's, in which Gaelic would be the language of
    the national assembly but not of the cantons or regions.

747. Snodaigh, Padraig. "Roots: the Achievement of Political Freedom in the 20th Century: a Study of Patterns." In Celtic League Annual, 50-58, Dublin: Celtic League, 1970.

Snodaigh notes the pattern of political struggle in Albania, Algeria, Laos, and other nations, and applies these lessons to the Celtic regions. He concludes that armed resistance is not always a matter of force but a matter of the willingness to fight to command respect from oppressive nations.

748. Stephens, Meic. Linguistic Minorities in Western Europe. Llandysul: Gomer, 1976. 796pp.

A fairly comprehensive account of the political and cultural struggles of European minorities. Over fifty minorities from 16 European nations are included. Scotland is treated in great detail. Includes excellent bibliography.

749. Williams, C.H., ed. National Separatism. Cardiff: U. of Wales, 1982. 317pp.

Explains the origin of national movements in Belgium, Quebec, Ireland, Wales, Scotland, and Euskada. D.N. MacIver writes on "The Paradox of Nationalism in Scotland."

ARTICLES

750. "Agricultural Correspondent." "The Soil of Scotland: Basis of a National Policy." Scottish Standard 1 (Sept. 1935): 19-20.

Denmark is presented as a model of a small state with a successful farming and land policy, one which might serve an independent Scotland well.

751. Campbell, J.L. "Norway: the Historical Background." Outlook (July 1936): 42-46.

Norway was independent from 872 to 1319, and regained its freedom after 486 years, in June, 1905. Campbell finds lessons for Scotland in Norway's freedom struggle.

752. Campbell, J.L. "Norway: the Results of Freedom-Part Two." Outlook (August 1936): 24-30.

Campbell finds in Norway a general flowering of culture. He views the work of Wergeland (1808-1845) and Welhaven (1807-1873) as especially relevant to cultural and political revival in Scotland.

753. Dass, Petter. "Reviving a Language: the Story of Frisian." Outlook (April 1936): 72-75.

Frisian as a model of language revival, with political lessons for Scotland.

754. Dass, Petter. "A Wind from the Skagerak: How the Norwegians Lost Their Language and Found it-New Norse and New Scots." Scottish Standard 1 (January 1936): 21-22.

A call for a New Scots language based on the successes of New Norse.

755. Dott, George. "A Lesson for Scotland: Catalonia under Home Rule." Scottish Standard 1 (September 1935): 5-6.

How Catalonia's self-sufficient economy could instruct Scotland, with emphasis on Catalonia's long preparation for Home Rule.

756. Gillies, Iain. "Scotland Among the Nations: Can Scotland Stand Alone?" Scots Independent (Feb. 1927): 1-2.

Concludes that Scotland's area, population, and revenue could allow Scotland to compete with successful small nations like Denmark and Norway.

757. Herdman, John. "Literature and National Self-Confidence" Catalyst 2 (Autumn 1969): 7-8.

Contrasts Irish Nationalism with Scottish, and hopes that Scotland, like Ireland, will fuel its political nationalism with a vigorous cultural and literary nationalism.

758. Illeasbuig, Gilleasbuig. "Our Language and our Music." Catalyst (Winter 1968): 25-26.

Traces the success of English culture in avoiding extinction in the 13th century, and encourages Scots to study the examples of Welsh and Hebrew.

759. Kennedy, T. "The Strangling of a Modern State." Modern Scot 1 (Summer 1930): 24-30.

A consideration of Ireland's economic problems and the challenges they pose for Home Rule in Scotland.

760. Lamont, Archie. "The Home Rule Island." National Weekly 4 (Jan. 12, 1952): 3.

The nature of government on the Isle of Man and its lessons for Scottish Home Rule.

761. Lamont, Archie. "The Home Rule Island." <u>National Weekly</u> 4 (Jan. 19, 1952): 4.

The revival of Manx language and culture and political lessons for Scotland.

762. Lamont, Archie. "Iceland Shows the Way." <u>National Weekly</u> 4 (June 7, 1952): 2.

How Iceland framed a Constitution and achieved a classless society. An example for Scotland, asks Lamont.

763. Lamont, Archie. "Iceland Shows the Way-Part Two." <u>National Weekly</u> 4 (June 14, 1952): 3.

How Iceland achieved a high standard of living along with a high level of culture.

764. Lamont, Archie. "Independence of Luxemburg." <u>National Weekly</u> 4 (Feb. 9, 1952): 3.

What Scotland can learn from this small self-governing nation.

765. Lamont, Archie. "Scotland and Norway." <u>National Weekly</u> 4 (March 29, 1952): 3.

Norway's lessons for Scotland in agriculture and land reform.

766. Lamont, Archie. "Scotland and Norway." <u>National Weekly</u> 4 (April 5, 1952): 4.

How Scotland might learn lessons from Norway in what Lamont terms "equalitarian democracy." Examples in fishing, forestry, and land reclamation.

767. Lamont, Archie. "Self-Government in the Channel Islands." <u>National Weekly</u> 4 (Feb. 23, 1952): 2.

How Jersey and Sark are governed, with lessons for Scottish Home Rule.

768. Lamont, Archie. "What Scotland Can Learn from Modern Ireland." <u>Scots Independent</u> (August 1936): 3.

Since Ireland's Free State status, Lamont finds vast improvements in agriculture, land reform, industry, and the quality of life. He believes that Scotland could do even better, given independence.

769. MacArthur, John. "Can Scotland Stand Alone?" Liberty 2 (Oct. 1921): 145-146.

MacArthur ranks nations of similar size by population and revenue, and finds that Scotland could easily compete in a world market and could compare favorably with nations such as Norway and Denmark.

770. MacColl, Malcolm. "The Road to Freedom." Scots Independent (March 1927): 1-2.

Other nations may provide examples of successful freedom struggles e.g. USA, Hungary 1840 --67, Italy, and Ireland.

771. MacDiarmid, Hugh. "Georgia and Scotland." National Weekly 3 (Dec. 9, 1950): 3.

A visit to Stalin's native Georgia in the USSR draws comparisons with Scotland, and MacDiarmid concludes that the Soviet Union has done far more to protect minority cultures than Britain has done.

772. MacDiarmid, Hugh. "Impressions of the USSR." Scots Review 11 (March 1951): 217-218.

Favorable impressions of the USSR. MacDiarmid is impressed with official encouragement of minority languages and literatures. Compares Stalin's Georgia with Scotland.

773. Mackenzie, Agnes Muir. "Another United Kingdom and its Changes." Today and Tomorrow 1 (Summer 1946): 16-20.

Norway's struggle for freedom and lessons for Scotland.

774. MacNeacail, H.C. "Lessons for Scotland from other Countries." Liberty 2 (Aug. 1921): 121-122.

Norway as a model for Scots independence; a discussion of its cultural and political revival.

775. MacNeacail, H.C. "Lessons for Scotland from other Countries." Liberty 2 (Sept. 1921): 138.

England's historical struggles to preserve language and nation and how Scotland can learn from those struggles.

776. MacNeacail, H.C. "Lessons for Scotland from Other Countries." Liberty 2 (October 1921): 149.

Lessons from Bulgaria and Bohemia.

777. MacNeacail, H.C. "Lessons for Scotland from other Countries." Liberty 2 (Nov. 1921): 173-174.

Hungary's fight for independence in the 19th century.

778. MacNeacail, H.C. "Lessons for Scotland from other Countries." Liberty 2 (Dec. 1921): 187-188.

MacNeacail concludes his series with a summary of the ways and means of achieving independence, and of the importance of language, folklore, and national education in giving birth to movements for self-rule.

779. Muirhead, Roland E. "A Glimpse of Norway: a Fine Example to Scotland." Scots Independent (September 1931): 167.

In 1931, Muirhead sees a progressive, prosperous Norway with no slums or unemployment, and with no war budget or National Debt. He finds many similarities with Scotland.

780. Nairne, Campbell. "Scotland and Belgium: How Flemish Writers Tackled their Language Problems." Scottish Standard 1 (Dec. 1935): 11-13.

How Flemish writers used a national language but retain an international outlook, with comparisons and lessons for Scotland.

781. Power, William. " A Tour in Sweden and Denmark." Forum 1 (August 1946): 6.

Denmark and Sweden as cultural and political models for Scotland.

782. Spence, Lewis. "Enthusiasm or Caution, Success or Ruin?" The Scottish Nation 1 (June 12, 1923): 4.

Spence criticizes Scottish Nationalists for their cautious inaction. He urges them to copy Irish, Polish, and Italian nationalists in their more dynamic approach.

783. Taylor, S.W. "The Language Question." Scottish Vanguard (April/May 1968): 10-11.

Taylor argues that politics can be international while culture can remain intensely national. He cites Albania as a successful example of this blend of nationalism and internationalism.

784. Thompson, Frank. "Expanding the Scope for Gaelic."
Books in Scotland (Winter 1978): 5-6.

Lessons from the revival of Faroese for Scotland.

785. Walkinshaw, Colin. "A Federal World." Scots Review
8 (March 1948): 169-170.

Switzerland's federal model and how it might serve
Scotland.

786. Wilson, John. "Norway's Example to Scotland." The
Scottish Patriot (Sept. 1905): 237.

Lessons from Norway in an article written in the year of
her independence.

787. Young, Douglas. "A Model Democracy: Switzerland's
Interest for Scotland." Scots Independent (August 1947): 1-2.

Swiss federalism and its possibilities in a free Scotland.

ORKNEY AND SHETLAND

Books and Pamphlets

788. Dowle, Martin. "The Birth and Development of the
Shetland Movement, 1977-1980." In The Scottish Government
Yearbook, 1981, edited by H.M. Drucker and N.L. Drucker,
203-221. Edinburgh: Paul Harris, 1980.

Dowle shows how an independent Scotland must decide
on some form of autonomy or Home Rule for the Shetlands.
He explains the "Shetland Movement" and its origins and
aims, its pragmatism and populism. A strong argument
for Shetland's case for important consideration under
a Scottish government.

789. Firth, Howie. "Communal Identity in Orkney and
Shetland." In The Radical Approach: Papers on an Independent
Scotland, edited by Gavin Kennedy, 27-32. Edinburgh:
Palingenesis Press, 1976.

The Shetlands and Orkneys have too long suffered
oppression and mis-management, argues Firth, and an
independent Scotland needs to study these islands very
carefully to avoid repeating the same mistakes. Firth
suggests some options, ranging from self-rule to
a type of federalism. In any case, he makes a good
argument for democracy in Scotland and her islands.

790. "Shetland and Devolution: the Labour View." In
Island Futures: Scottish Devolution and Shetland's
Constitutional Alternatives, edited by Roy Gronneberg,
52-57. Sandwick: Thuleprint, 1978.

   Presents in detail the Labour Party's plans for
   Shetland in a devolved Scotland.

791. Gronneberg, Roy., ed. Island Futures: Scottish
Devolution and Shetland's Constitutional Alternatives.
Sandwick: Thuleprint, 1978. 79pp.

   A thorough discussion of devolution for Shetland from
   many points of view. All political parties are
   represented and pro and con views are given. Distinctive
   features of Shetland life and culture are discussed
   and special problems are considered. The ideas and aims
   of "The Shetland Group" are presented.

792. Grimond, Jo. "Devolution, Democracy, and the Threat of
Overgovernment." In Island Futures: Scottish Devolution and
Shetland's Constitutional Alternatives, edited by Roy
Gronneberg, 35-41. Sandwick: Thuleprint, 1978.

   Grimond, a Liberal Party Member of Parliament for
   Shetland and Orkney for many years, examines the
   possibility that devolution for Scotland and then
   Shetland might result in costly and conflicting
   bureaucracy and overgovernment. He suggests in this
   chapter how the Shetlands might avoid this while
   maintaining democracy in the islands.

793. Halcrow, Grace. "Devolution-the Tory View." In
Island Futures: Scottish Devolution and Shetland's
Constitutional Alternatives, edited by Roy Gronneberg,
44-45. Sandwick: Thuleprint, 1978.

   Halcrow states the Tory position that devolution for
   Scotland and Shetland will make for even more
   bureaucracy and waste than ever before. She does
   suggest alternatives for Shetland government at the
   local level.

794. Irvine, James. "The Shetland Group." In Island Futures:
Scottish Devolution and Shetland's Constitutional Alternatives.
edited by Roy Gronneberg, 57-62. Sandwick: Thuleprint, 1978.

   The aims and influence of the important Shetland Group
   founded by 14 people from all political persuasions in
   Shetland. Since its founding in 1977, it has had
   considerable influence in shaping political opinion.
   The article explains the significance of the "Shetland
   Group."

795. Macartney, Allan. "Routes to Island Autonomy?" In
The Scottish Government Yearbook 1983, edited by David
McCrone, 140-160. Edinburgh: EUSG, 1982.

   The aims, background, and nature of the quest for
   autonomy or devolution within Scotland by Orkney and
   Shetland.

796. MacDiarmid, Hugh. "Faroese Holiday." In At the Sign
of the Thistle: A Collection of Essays. London: Nott, 1934,
125-147.

   A trip to the Faroe Islands provides MacDiarmid with a
   successful example of a reclaimed and unified organic
   culture. He feels the Faroes could provide an example
   to Shetland.

797. MacDiarmid, Hugh. "Life in the Shetland Islands." In
At the Sign of the Thistle: A Collection of Essays. London:
Nott, 1934, 148-163.

   The deprivation and cultural decay MacDiarmid sees in
   the Shetlands can be altered in the same way as the
   Faroes, argues MacDiarmid.

798. Manson, T.M. "The Urge for Autonomy." In Island Futures:
Scottish Devolution and Shetland's Constitutional
Alternatives, edited by Roy Gronneberg, 12-18. Sandwick:
Thuleprint, 1978.

   A sketch of Shetland's political past and the features
   of life there that will require special political
   sensitivity on the part of Scottish government.

799. Massie, Allan. "A Distinctive Culture?" In Island
Futures: Scottish Devolution and Shetland's Constitutional
Alternatives, edited by Roy Gronneberg, 26-31. Sandwick:
Thuleprint, 1978.

   Massie explores the traits of the Shetland character
   and culture that make it a unique blend of many
   traditions, especially Norse ones. A Scottish
   government should understand the non-Scottish features
   of Shetland life.

800. Nairn, Tom. "The Shetland Problem." In Island Futures:
Scottish Devolution and Shetland's Constitutional
Alternatives, edited by Roy Gronneberg, 18-24. Sandwick:
Thuleprint, 1978.

   Nairn analyzes the problems of governing Shetland in
   light of the broader relationship between Scotland and
   England.

801. Shetland Islands Council. "Statement on the Scotland
Bill." In Island Futures: Scottish Devolution and Shetland's
Constitutional Alternatives, edited by Roy Gronneberg,
32-35. Sandwick: Thuleprint, 1978.

   The official response to the Scotland Bill, with a
   request for special consideration for Shetland.

802. Spens, Michael. "Special Status for Shetland." In
Island Futures: Scottish Devolution and Shetland's
Constitutional Alternatives, edited by Roy Gronneberg,
45-52. Sandwick: Thuleprint, 1978.

   The varieties of government available to Shetland, its
   options under devolution, and the unique features of
   Shetland life that require special status by a
   Scottish government.

ORKNEY AND SHETLAND

Articles

803. Firth, Howie. "Whither Orkney and Shetland?"
Question (March 1976): 8-10.

   Why a new Scotland will have to also consider claims
   by Orkney and Shetland to more democracy in light of
   North Sea oil discoveries.

804. Graham, Lawrence. "A Shetlander Speaks." Scots Review
8 (August 1947): 51.

   A review of Shetland history and its past economic and
   political troubles; also, its need for democracy,
   devolution, or independence.

805. Murray, Walter. "Orkney and Home Rule." Scottish
Home Rule 5 (September 1924): 23.

   Problems in governing Orkney and the necessity of
   a Scottish Home Rule government's special handling
   of those problems.

806. Spens, Michael. "Island Politics: Greenland, Aland,
Faroe, Shetland." Bulletin of Scottish Politics (Autumn 1980):
51-61.

   A comparison of Shetland with these other islands, and
   how progressive self-rule in Shetland would benefit
   Scotland and socialism. Self-rule for Shetland would
   also pave the way for more democracy throughout
   Britain, argues Spens.

10.

1980–   : QUESTIONS

> From old Scots nobles in the rear
> Of each new upstart English Peer
> And rouping Parliament robes next year
>   Deliver us, Lord.
>   "A Litanie Anent the Union"
>   Anonymous, 1707

In the twentieth century, Scottish Nationalism has been nothing if not resilient. The 1980's will test that resiliency. Will Conservative government kill Scottish independence or make the self-rule movement more determined? Will Gaelic and Scots survive the century? Will left-wing nationalists finally mobilize Scotland's working class? Will Scottish Nationalism, so long defined by its caution and non-violence resort to more violent means as the economy worsens? Meanwhile, Scotland's culture appears very healthy. Poets, musicians, political theorists and other Scots are especially creative, whether out of anger or futility, or both. Many Scottish writers find their art tied to Scotland's own status. Whatever happens elsewhere, the decade in Scotland will not be a complacent or quiet one.

BOOKS AND PAMPHLETS

807. Allen, Chris. "Governing North Britain: Recent Studies of Scottish Politics." In The Scottish Government Yearbook 1983, edited by David McCrone, 217-227. Edinburgh: EUSG, 1982.

A bibliographic essay on eight important books appearing in 1980-82, some of which deal with Scottish Nationalism.

808. Bochel, John.; Denver, David.; and Macartney, Allan. The Referendum Experience: Scotland 1979. Aberdeen: Aberdeen U. Press, 1981, 210pp.

Detailed study of the Scottish referendum of 1979. Analysis of the press, the campaigns, posters, cartoons, etc. A chronology included. The authors clarify and explain the confusion surrounding the referendum. A chapter on the Welsh experience. A thorough work.

809. Burrows, Bernard., and Denton, Geoffrey. Devolution or Federalism: Options for a United Kingdom. London: MacMillan, 1980. 94pp.

A complete study of federalism, its limits and potential, its possibilities in the United Kingdom, and its successes and failures elsewhere. Special attention given to a Scotland within a federal system. Federalism has long been an option for Scotland, and is part of official Liberal Party policy.

810. Campaign for a Scottish Assembly. Blueprint for Scotland: Discussion Paper. Glasgow: Campaign for a Scottish Assembly, 1982. 8pp.

Explains this movement which works for a broad coalition of all parties and individuals to unite to work for a National Assembly or Parliament for Scotland.

811. Campbell, James., ed. New Edinburgh Review Anthology. Edinburgh: Polygon, 1982. 203pp.

Fiction, articles, criticism and poetry taken from the New Edinburgh Review. International, but with strong Scottish emphasis. Of special interest: Tom Nairn on "After the Referendum," and James Young: "The Clans and the Kailyard."

812. Carney, John. "Regions in Crisis: Accumulation, Regional Problems and Crisis Formation." In Regions in Crisis, edited by John Carney, 22-59. London: Croom Helm, 1980.

Carney analyzes Scotland's economy. He sees devolution as an unsuccessful scheme to prevent radical solutions to what he terms Scotland's "outdated" economy.

813.   Carney, John., ed. <u>Regions in Crisis: New Perspectives</u> <u>in European Regional Theory</u>. London: Croom Helm, 1980. 179pp.

With France as a model, the authors explore the uneven development of European regions with regard to invest- ment. They also consider monopolies, employment, emigration, and central authority. Scotland is dealt with in chapter 2: "Regions in Crisis: Accumulation, Regional Problems and Crisis Formation."

814.   Carty, Tony. "Scottish Legal Culture and the Withering Away of the State: A Study in MacCormick's Nationalism." <u>Cencrastus</u> (Autumn 1983): 5-9.

A thorough explanation of the origins and implications of the political theories of Neil MacCormick, Professor of Public Law at Edinburgh University. MacCormick is a leading figure in the Scottish National Party and son of John MacCormick.

815.   Daiches, David., ed. <u>A Companion to Scottish Culture</u>. New York: Holmes and Meier, 1983. 441pp.

An encyclopedic work covering all aspects of Scottish culture, with some explanation of Scottish politics. Comprehensive treatment, ranging from sports and myth to literature and philosophy. Useful for sources and bibliography.

816.   Drucker, Henry. "The Curious Incident: Scottish Party Competition Since 1979." In <u>The Scottish Government Yearbook</u>, edited by David McCrone, 16-32. Edinburgh: EUSG, 1982.

Analysis of the major parties since 1979. The SNP is seen as weak and demoralized and Drucker concludes that it is not a serious political force at present.

817.   Drucker, H.M., ed. <u>John P. Mackintosh on Scotland</u>. London: Longmans, 1982. 232pp.

Mackintosh , scholar and Labour Member of Parliament, died in 1978, after many years of public service. Besides a chronology of Mackintosh's life, much attention is given to his articles and writings on devolution, regional and local government, and democracy for Scotland. Many of the contributors place Mackintosh within the great tradition of Scottish writers and politicians who have brought more democracy to British politics. Mackintosh has had great influence on political thought in the United Kingdom.

818. Drucker, H.M., and Drucker, N.L., eds. The Scottish
Government Yearbook-1980. Edinburgh: Paul Harris, 1979, 319pp.

   Topics include: fishing, industry, energy, the
   referendum. The usual excellent reference section with
   30 page bibliography of articles and books on Scottish
   politics, including nationalism.

819. Drucker, H.M., and Drucker, N.L., eds. The Scottish
Government Yearbook-1981. Edinburgh: Paul Harris, 1980.
330pp. bibl.

   Contains results of opinion polls and views on
   devolution and independence. Facts on the "Shetland
   Movement," and on the social structure of modern Scotland.
   Bibliography of books and articles on Scottish politics,
   including nationalism.

820. Drucker, H.M., and Drucker, N.L., eds. The Scottish
Government Yearbook-1982. Edinburgh: Paul Harris, 1981. 343
pp. bibl.

   Chapters on recession, unemployment, industrial training,
   the National Health Service, and the environment.
   Extensive bibliography on the year's articles and
   books on Scottish politics, including Scottish Nationalism.

821. Durkacz, Victor. The Decline of the Celtic Languages.
Edinburgh: John Donald, 1983. 200pp. bibl.

   A general account of the history and neglect and decline
   of the Celtic languages, with special emphasis on Gaelic
   and Welsh. Durkacz avoids simple answers for their decline
   and studies the effects of religion and education.
   An excellent 25 page bibliography is included.

822. Hart, Tom. "Transport Policy." In Scotland 1980: the
Economics of Self Government, edited by Donald MacKay,
158-172. Edinburgh: Q Press, 1977.

   Hart envisions a fully integrated transport system for
   a free Scotland, combining the best features of public
   and private transport.

823. Harvie, Christopher. No Gods and Precious Few Heroes:
Scotland 1914-1980. London: Edward Arnold, 1981. 182pp.

   Divides into three periods: 1911-1922; 1922-1964; 1964-
   1980. This history covers important years for Scottish
   Nationalism. Harvie investigates closely the link
   between economics and the demand for change in government.

824.   Heald, David. Financing Devolution Within the UK: A
Study of Lessons from Failure. Canberra: The Australian
National University, 1980. 142pp.

An academic study of the economic principles and
realities of devolution proposals in the U.K. in the
1970's. Heald concentrates heavily on the method of
devolved taxes and taxation schemes necessary to fund
devolution.

825.   Lythe, Charlotte. "The Scottish Economy in 1980." In
Scotland 1980: the Economics of Self Government, edited by
Donald MacKay, 19-36. Edinburgh: Q Press, 1977.

Lythe examines the present in order to forecast the
future. North Sea oil and gas production results in
variables that make an independent Scotland's economy
difficult to forecast, concludes Lythe.

826.   Lythe, Charlotte, and Majmudar, Madhavi. The
Renaissance of the Scottish Economy. London: George Allen
and Unwin, 1982. 224pp.

An appraisal of the Scottish economy over the past 25
years, with much attention paid to its future. Devolution
is discussed as well as problems posed by self-government.
The authors do conclude that Scotland's economy is
inseparable from that of the United Kingdom. To
support this prognosis, many tables and charts are
included. A thorough study of all aspects of Scotland's
economy and its potential. Bibliography. Their
conclusions are important for Scottish Nationalists.

827.   McCrone, David. The Scottish Government Yearbook-1983.
Edinburgh: EUSG, 1982. 302pp.

See "Governing North Britain..." by Chris Allen.
Contains a 384 item bibliography on Scottish politics.

828.   McEwen, John. Who Owns Scotland: a Study in Land
Ownership. Edinburgh: Edinburgh University, 1981. 120pp.

The urgent need for land reform in Scotland is
examined. Abuses by absentee owners, and the forms of
control by corporations and government agencies.
"Landlordism in Scotland: the Top 100 Landowners" is a
key feature of the work. McEwen's study is an
important source for understanding the complexities of
land ownership in Scotland. A powerful argument for
land reform and resources management in an independent
Scotland.

829. McGilvray, J.W. "Economic Policy and Management." In
Scotland 1980: the Economics of Self Government, edited by
Donald MacKay, 48-61. Edinburgh: Q Press, 1977.

    Self-government, argues McGilvray, won't solve
    two major problems in Scotland: low economic growth and
    high unemployment.

830. MacKay, G.A. "Energy Policy." In Scotland 1980: the
Economics of Self-Government, edited by Donald MacKay, 145-
167. Edinburgh: Q Press, 1977.

    MacKay hopes an independent Scotland would use less
    nuclear power, more coal,oil, and gas, and devise a
    more flexible but consistent policy than the present one.
    He argues for more exploration into alternative energy
    sources.

831. Maxwell, Stephen. Scotland, Multinationals and the
Third World. Edinburgh: Mainstream, 1982. 158pp.

    Maxwell notes the heavy investment in Scotland of
    American, English, and other nations' multinationals.
    He draws parallels with the Third World, and urges
    Scots to study the record of multinationals in the
    Third World.

832. Miller, William., Brand, Jack., and Jordan, Maggie.
Oil and the Scottish Voter 1974-1979. London: Social Science
Research Council, 1980. 111pp.

    In-depth study of the relationship between North Sea oil
    revenues, and the Scottish voters' attitudes to devolution
    or independence. 1974 and 1979 are compared. Short
    bibliography.

833. Mitchison, Rosalind., ed. The Roots of Nationalism:
Studies in Northern Europe. Edinburgh: John Donald, 1980.
175pp.

    Collection of papers presented at a Conference on
    Nationalism held in Wales in 1979. Ireland, Iceland,
    Denmark, Finland, Norway, and other nations were
    discussed.

834. Nairn, Tom. "After the Referendum." In The New
Edinburgh Review Anthology, edited by James Campbell,53-70.
Edinburgh: Polygon, 1982.

    Analysis of the referendum of 1979 and its aftermath.
    Nairn thinks the defeat of the Scotland Bill may
    actually hasten the end of the United Kingdom, by
    revealing key failings of the democratic system. He
    concludes: "the question of radicalising the Scottish
    movement...assumes great urgency as well as great
    desirability."

835. Nairn, Tom. The Break-Up of Britain: Crisis and
Neo-Colonialism. London: Verson, 1981. 404pp.

Nairn gives an in-depth analysis of the modern
British state, with emphasis on nationalism.
Some chapter titles indicate Nairn's many arguments and
themes: "The Twilight of the British State;" "Scotland
and Europe;" "Old and New Scottish Nationalism;"
"English Nationalism: the Case of Enoch Powell."
Nairn applies his knowledge of European socialism and
Marxism to Scottish Nationalism, and defines true
internationalism. A knowledge of Marxist theory would
help the reader interpret this widely discussed book.
This 1981 edition is an expansion of his 1977 edition
and includes an important summary and prognosis.
Nairn is editor of the Bulletin of Scottish Politics.

836. Simpson, David. The Economics of Self-Government in
Scotland. Edinburgh: SNP Research Dept., 1982. 16pp.

Examines two decades of the management of the Scottish
economy. Presents alternatives to the present system.
Studies the impact of North Sea oil on Scotland's
future. Concludes that Scotland would gain materially
from independence in the long run.

837. Simpson, David. "Performance, Efficiency and Growth."
In Scotland 1980: the Economics of Self Government, edited
by Donald MacKay, 37-47. Edinburgh: Q Press, 1977.

Simpson analyzes Scotland's economy over the past 25
years. He argues that an independent Scotland would have
to have a very coherent economic plan in order to halt
stagnation.

838. Snyder, Louis L. Global Mini-Nationalisms: Autonomy
or Independence. Westport, Connecticut: Greenwood Press,
1982. 326pp.

A thorough study of nationalism and its various
historical and geographical manifestations. Includes
many definitions and case studies. Chapters on Scotland
and Wales and movements throughout Europe, Asia, and
North America. Useful notes and bibliography.

839. Snyder, Louis L. "British Devolution I: Scottish
Nationalism." In Global Mini-Nationalisms. Westport, Conn.
Greenwood, 1982, 25-39.

Traces the development of Scottish Nationalism, the
language question, the distinct features of Scottish
culture, the causes of the popularity of the SNP, and
the problem of Shetland.

840. Snyder, Louis L. "Nationalism and its Peripheries."
In Global Mini-Nationalisms. Westport, Conn. Greenwood, 1982,
1-10.

   On the persistence of nationalism, its relation to
   communism, the strength of its urge to political
   independence, theories and methods of research into
   nationalism, and problems of definition and classification.

841. Snyder, Louis L. "Postscript in Decalogue." In
Global Mini-Nationalisms. Westport, Conn. Greenwood, 1982,
251-256.

   Conclusions from the book: nationalism can be a force for
   good or evil; it represents a struggle between authority
   and decentralization; its unpredictable, emotional,
   and resilient. This chapter summarizes Snyder's findings.

842. Young, James D. "The Clans and the Kailyard." In The
New Edinburgh Review Anthology, edited by James Campbell,
71-79. Edinburgh: Polygon, 1982.

   An international gathering of the clans in Scotland
   prompts Young to review the Highland Clearances of the
   19th century. He argues that most writers on the
   Clearances ignore the part that the dispossessed
   Highlanders played in industrial agitation. Young calls
   for more careful study of the Highlands from a
   socialist point of view.

                          ARTICLES

843. Bain, Dougie. "Doing it Ourselves." Bulletin of
Scottish Politics (Autumn 1980): 40-46.

   Bain explains the failure of the Scotland Act and
   the confusion surrounding the referendum.

844. Bain, Doug. "Where Now for the Scottish Left?" Radical
Scotland (Aug./Sept. 1983): 14-16.

   Analyzes the failures and weaknesses of the Scottish
   left. Predicts the "emergence of a new, national
   left in Scotland." The Socialist Society "represents
   a coming together of the new Left and Nationalist Left"
   in a new politics, embracing feminism, ecology, etc.

845. Beveridge, A.C. "A Case of Hardened Arteries: Scottish
Political Culture." Cencrastus (Summer 1981): 14-15.

Beveridge calls for the integration of research,
activity, theory, and public life to help bridge the
gap between information and theory in post-referendum
Scotland.

846. Black, David. "What Attitude Should We Have Towards
the Union?" Chapman (February 1983): 2-5.

Reviews the Union since 1707. The Union is seen as
necessary for that time, but equally unnecessary for
the present. Black compares the Union to a "stale
marriage" with divorce as the only solution.

847. Brand, Jack. "Educating Nationalists." Bulletin of
Scottish Politics (Autumn 1980): 36-40.

Brand explains why Scottish Nationalist support
jumped from 2.4% of the electorate in 1964 to 30.4%
in 1974. He concludes that the future success of the
Scottish National Party depends on the support of the
urban working class and the trade unions.

848. Brand, Jack. "A National Assembly." Crann Tara (Spring
1981): 15.

Brand writes on how a Scottish Assembly must have full
powers to attack Scotland's economic problems. He calls
for all parties and individuals in Scotland to unite in
support of a Scottish Assembly.

849. Burke, Ruth Hamilton. "The Scotland-UN Committee."
Keltica (1983): 55.

The history of the aims of the Scottish-UN Committee,
which believes the mismanaged referendum "violated the
Scottish people's right to self-determination as
guaranteed by the UN Covenant on Civil and Political
Rights."

850. Carty, Tony. "Independence and the Scottish Political
Imagination." Cencrastus (1983): 26-28.

A reconsideration by the author of his 1978 book,
Power and Manoeuvreability: the international
implications of an independent Scotland.

851. Craig, Cairns. "Peripheries." Cencrastus (Summer 1982):
3-8.

A consideration of political and cultural "peripheries"
and their vitality expressed through literature.

852. Dunion, Kevin., ed. "In the Red Corner." Radical
Scotland (Aug./Sept. 1983): 7-8.

  Reports on a conference held by the Scottish Socialist
  Society, Radical Scotland, and the Glasgow Fabian Society.
  Dunion notes the confusion and disagreement among the
  Scottish left about an independent Scotland.

853. Dunion, Kevin., ed. "Recipes for Socialism." Radical
Scotland (Aug./Sept. 1983): 9-11.

  An interview with Robin Cook, Labour Member of Parliament
  for Livingston, Scotland. Cook explains his recent
  endorsement of federalism and devolution.

854. Dunion, Kevin. "SNP: 79 into 83 Won't Go?" Scottish
Marxist (Spring 1983): 10-11.

  An account of the socialist "79 Group" and their reasons
  for withdrawl from the SNP, and of their aim for an
  independent socialist Scotland.

855. Durkacz, Victor. "Imperialism and Celtic Culture."
Cencrastus (Spring 1980): 22-23.

  An historical account of the decline of Gaelic culture
  in Scotland. Durkacz concludes that Celtic Scotland is
  not a "museum piece" but is "a viable vernacular with a
  firm foothold in Scotland's future."

856. Easton, Norman. "Was the State Behind Tartan Terrorism?"
Crann Tara (New Year, 1982): 18-20.

  Sketches Scottish Nationalist violence, real and alleged,
  its treatment by the press, and speculates on the
  possible existence of a "political martyr cult."

857. Foulkes, George. "Labour for an Assembly." Crann Tara
(Winter 1981): 7.

  Reasons why only the Labour Party can possibly produce
  a Scottish Parliament.

858. Harvie, Christopher. "Beyond Bairn's Play: a New
Agenda for Scottish Politics." Cencrastus (Autumn 1982): 11-
14.

  A re-assessment of Harvie's own Scotland and Nationalism
  (1977). Harvie lists needed improvements for Scotland
  in education, communications, and public health.

859. Harvie, Christopher. "Labour and Scottish Government: the Age of Tom Johnston." <u>The Bulletin of Scottish Politics</u> (Spring 1981): 1-20.

>   Tom Johnston's tenure of Secretary of State for Scotland is evaluated. Johnston was appointed in February, 1941, and many Scottish Nationalists and socialists had high hopes for his abilities. Harvie finds Johnston's achievements "ambiguous" and "short on innovation."

860. Hechter, Michael. "Internal Colonialism Revisited." <u>Cencrastus</u> (Autumn 1982): 8-11.

>   Hechter evaluates his major work and finds it "not so much incorrect as it is incomplete" and believes more answers to his original questions will be forthcoming when more data is gathered.

861. Heller, Nick. "Beyond Federalism." <u>Radical Scotland</u> (Aug./Sept. 1983): 12-13.

>   Heller is Chairperson for the Young Scottish Liberals. He points out that federalism has always meant different things to the Scots and English. Under a United Kingdom federalism, Scotland would only be treated as a region, while Scots would prefer Scotland to be treated as a sovereign state. He challenges the official Liberal Party support for federalism for Scotland. Heller then argues for independence with a "common forum." He concludes: "The United Kingdom can never operate successfully as a federal state from the Scottish point of view because England would dominate numerically, economically and politically."

862. Hepburn, Ian. "The Foulkes Memorandum." <u>Radical Scotland</u> (Aug. Sept. 1983): 18-19.

>   Disclosure of a memorandum from George Foulkes, Labour Member of Parliament for Carrick, Cumnock, and Doon Valley, urging boycotts, legal and parliamentary means, strikes, petitions, etc. to force a national plebiscite on Home Rule or devolution for Scotland. This proposal was to be considered by Labour's Scottish Executive.

863. Hubbard, Tom. "Re-evaluation: R.B. Cunninghame-Graham." <u>Cencrastus</u> (Spring 1982): 27-30.

>   An appraisal of the political life and writings of R.B. Cunninghame-Graham (1852-1936).

864. Hunter, James. "Year of the Emigre." <u>Bulletin of Scottish Politics</u> (Spring 1981): 56-62.

>   Comments on the "Year of the Scot," established to honour overseas Scots with clan links. He examines why and how Irish and Scots emigres differ in political attitudes to their countries.

865. Keating, Michael. "Labour and Scottish Nationalism: an Update." Cencrastus (Spring 1983): 29-31.

Keating evaluates his book, which appeared in 1980. He finds that Labour support for Home Rule has had various forms, many of them opportunistic.

866. Kerevan, George. "Labourism Revisited." Chapman 7 (July 1983): 25-31.

Kerevan defines Scotland's "Labourism"-a reformist, but not radical tradition that has actually impeded socialism and democracy in Scotland. He pays special attention to 1915-1919. He argues that the end of "labourism" will benefit Scotland and hopes for a broad coalition that will demand self-rule for Scotland. This coalition should "emulate the tactics of the Irish Home Rule movement."

867. Kerevan, George. "Whither Scotland?" Bulletin of Scottish Politics (Autumn 1980): 23-30.

The writer challenges the nationalist left in Scotland to mobilize the working class vote and to advocate true and radical socialism.

868. Law, T.S. "The National Community." Chapman 7 (July 1983): 93-97.

Law argues for a cultural and political renewal in Scotland.

869. MacArthur, Colin. "Breaking the Signs: Scotch Myths as Cultural Struggle." Cencrastus (Winter 1981-82): 21-25.

An interesting study of postcard themes reveals several myths relating to the kilt, Scots parsimony, militarism, the romantic Highlands, etc. MacArthur says that these myths must be understood, exposed, and replaced by more constructive ones.

870. MacKillop, Andrew. "The EEC, Energy, and the Celtic Nations." Keltica (1983): 11-15.

MacKillop, an energy consultant, surveys the energy scene in the Celtic areas of Europe. Control over dwindling resources of oil, gas, coal, uranium, and near-monopolies on hydro and nuclear power will give regions like Scotland much political bargaining power in the future.

871. MacMillan, Duncan. "Scotland and the Art of Nationalism." Cencrastus (Winter 1980-81): 33-35.

A painter links political alienation to artistic alienation, and challenges the outside control of the arts in minority cultures.

872. McMillan, Joyce. "The Predicament of the Scottish
Writer." Chapman 7 (July 1983): 68-71.

How Scottish writers can and must use their political
and cultural situation to improve their art.

873. McNaughton, Adam. "Songs for a Scottish Republic."
Chapman 7 (Spring 1982): 30-38.

An issue devoted to the work of Morris Blythman
("Thurso Berwick") and his songs, poetry, and other
writings and activities in support of an independent
Scottish socialist republic.

874. MacNeacail, Aonghas. "Rage Against the Dying Of."
Chapman 7 (July 1983): 54-58.

A Gaelic writer reveals the problems of writing in
Gaelic for a limited audience. He concludes; "choosing
our native language to express our deepest thoughts is a
necessary political act."

875. Maxwell, Stephen. "Encounter with the Third World."
Cencrastus (Winter 1980-81): 10-12.

Maxwell notes how Scotland at one time benefited from
British exploitation of the Third World through its
share of Empire. Now, he argues, Scotland's situation
at the hands of multinationals parallels many Third
World countries. Study and understanding of the Third
World would thus aid Scotland's self-awareness.

876. Maxwell, Stephen. "No Public Place." Chapman 7
(Spring 1980): 2-7.

An article on the paralysis of the Scottish middle class
and its inability to see politics as part of Scottish
culture as a whole, and its torn allegiances.

877. Maxwell, Stephen. "Scotland and the British Crisis."
Bulletin of Scottish Politics (Autumn 1980): 62-68.

Maxwell ponders the complete failure of the Labour Party
and the left to solve the great social problems in
Scotland. The Scottish left should counter that failed
socialism with a positive and radical socialism of its
own, he states.

878. Mulholland, Robert. "Nationalism vs.Imperialism."
Radical Scotland (Oct./Nov. 1983): 19.

Defines imperialism and give examples of its workings in
Scotland and Ireland. Discusses complicity of socialists
in this by "languishing in British parties." Argues for
a nationalism that will promote socialism and challenge
British imperialism.

879. Neill, William. "Fetch Ony Native Scottish Bird."
Chapman 7 (July 1983): 14-17.

    A writer's selection of language and how it defines his
    "Scottishness."

880. Paterson, Lindsay. "New Directions for Labour."
Bulletin of Scottish Politics (Autumn 1980): 30-36.

    Decentralization as a key task for the Labour Party in
    its attempt to form proper policies for governing
    Scotland.

881. Purves, Graham. "Devolution: Once More with Feeling."
Radical Scotland (Feb./March 1983): 15-16.

    Purves believes all anti-Tory parties should unite in
    their efforts to form a Scottish government that
    represents the wishes of the anti-Tory Scottish
    majority.

882. Ross, Jim. "Scottish Government in Stagnation."
Radical Scotland (Oct./Nov. 1983): 18-19.

    On the Conservative Party's shortage of Scottish
    Conservatives to fill key posts to run Scotland.

883. Ross, Raymond J. "Thurso Berwick: Solidarity without
Compromise." Chapman 7 (Spring 1982): 10-17.

    Further tribute to the late Morris Blythman who wrote
    under the pseudonym "Thurso Berwick." Article notes
    his involvement with the Campaign for Nuclear
    Disarmament and with Scottish Nationalism and socialism.

884. Skirrow, Gillian. "Woman, Women and Scotland: Scotch
Reels and Political Perspectives." Cencrastus (1983): 3-6.

    A discussion of the image of women in Scottish film.
    Many of these roles stress the need for women to
    define themselves as both Scots and women, a doubly
    difficult task, observes Ms. Skirrow.

885. Steel, Gordon. "Are the Scots a Nation? Wha Us?"
Crann Tara (Autumn 1980): 18-19.

    Steel argues that Scotland already has all the
    important characteristics of nationhood and that a
    Scottish Parliament would easily reflect those
    national characteristics.

886. Storrar, Willie. "No Room, No Birth, Some Magi."
Cencrastus (Autumn 1982): 3-8.

A useful discussion of important Scottish political
writers of the 1970's including John P. Mackintosh,
Tom Nairn, Christopher Harvie, and Stephen Maxwell, and
how they have paved the way for political discussion and
change in the 1980's.

887. Sutherland, Ian. "The Angry Scots." New Society (June
18, 1981): 469-470.

Overview of social problems in Scotland, Scottish
militancy, civil service radicalism, the power of the
communists, and the possible social unrest that may
fuel the movement for independence in Scotland in the
1980's.

888. Thomson, Christopher. "The Anglicization of Scots Law."
Cencrastus (Spring 1983): 2-5.

Thomson gives instances of the uniqueness of Scots Law and
how some of its best features are eroded by Parliament.
An essay on the current unsatisfactory legal
relationship between Scots Law and Westminster.

889. Toms, Duncan. "Tom Murray: 2nd August 1900-8th Feb.
1983," Radical Scotland (Aug./Sept. 1983): 20-22.

Murray's long and varied political career. The article
traces his involvement with the Independent Labour Party
and the Scottish Home Rule Association. Murray left the
Communist Party in 1965 and argued for self-rule for
a socialist Scotland.

890. Turnbull, Ronald, and Beveridge, Craig. "Philosophy
and Autonomy." Cencrastus (Summer 1980): 2-4.

The authors argue for a broader philosophical base for
Scottish Nationalism and emphasize the need for a
stronger link between Scotland and the Continent. At
present, they observe that Scottish education is
Anglicized and therefore tied to an English outlook
and not an international one. Scotland should thus
attempt to restore its European and international outlook.

891. Whyte, Christopher. "Out of a Predicament." Radical
Scotland (Oct./Nov. 1983): 20-21.

Reports on the July, 1983 meeting held to discuss
the peculiar dilemma facing Scottish writers and poets.
Whyte reports evidence of a strongly felt relationship
between culture and politics in Scotland.

892. Wilkie, James. "The Government of Scotland in Light of the Scotland Act." <u>Keltica</u> (1983): 56-59.

The Scotland Act and the referendum prompt Wilkie to study the constitutionality of the Scots Union with England, and he concludes that 14 of the original 25 articles of Union have been replaced or altered without Scotland's consent.

893. Wilson, Gordon. "Nationalism for Nationalists." <u>Radical Scotland</u> (June/July 1983): 16-17.

The legal procedure for Scots MP withdrawl from Westminster, under the aegis of a Scottish Convention which would support self-government for Scotland from a pluralistic point of view.

894. Wolfe, Billy. "Clear Stream Ahead." <u>Radical Scotland</u> (Oct./Nov. 1983): 9-11.

Skepticism about Scotland ever achieving self-rule under Westminster. Urges the setting up of Scots Parliament and poses questions concerning Unilateral Declaration of Independence.

APPENDIX I.

SOME LEADING SCOTTISH NATIONALIST JOURNALS OF THE TWENTIETH CENTURY

1900-1939

Fiery Cross
Free Man
Guth na Bliadhna
Modern Scot
Outlook

Reveille
Scots Independent
Scottish Nation
Scottish Standard
Thistle

1940-1959

Forum
Forward Scotland
Lion Rampant
Nationalist

National Weekly
New Alliance
Scots Independent
Scots Socialist
Scottish News and Comment

1960-1974

Catalyst
Crann Tara
Question
Schiltrom

Scots Independent
Scottish International
Scottish Vanguard
Sgian Dubh

1975-1979

Calgacus
Crann Tara
Question

Scots Independent
Sgian Dubh

1980-

Bulletin of Scottish Politics	Radical Scotland
Crann Tara	Scots Independent
National Liberation	Scottish Marxist

CURRENT SCOTTISH PERIODICALS FREQUENTLY HAVING ARTICLES ON
SCOTTISH NATIONALISM

Books in Scotland	New Edinburgh Review
Bulletin of Scottish Politics	New Shetlander
Cencrastus	Radical Scotland
Chapman	Scottish Journal of Sociology
Gairm	Scottish Marxist
National Liberation	Scottish Worker

GENERAL BRITISH PERIODICALS OFTEN HAVING ARTICLES ON
SCOTTISH POLITICS OR ON SCOTTISH NATIONALISM

British Journal of Political Science	New Left Review
Contemporary Review	New Outlook
Economist	New Society
Futures	New Statesman
Government and Opposition	Parliamentary Affairs
Journal of Contemporary History	Political Quarterly
Listener	Public Administration
New Europe	Spectator

APPENDIX II.

CULTURAL AND POLITICAL ORGANIZATIONS

An Comann Gaidhealach. Abertarff House, Inverness IV1 1EU, Scotland.

> Established 1891, "it is a non-party political, non-sectarian fellowship striving for the renewal of Scotland's oldest language, Scotland's pedigree - Gaelic."

Assembly of the Fourth World. 24 Abercorn Place, London NW8, England.

> "For small nations, small communities, and the Human Spirit."

Campaign for a Scottish Assembly. Chairperson, Jack Brand, 17 Kew Terrace, Glasgow G12 OTE, Scotland.

> "Committed to the establishment of a Scottish Assembly or Parliament."

Celtic League. 9 Br. Cnoc Sion, Dublin 9, Eire.

> Established 1961 to aid "the struggle of the six Celtic nations to secure and win their political, cultural, social and economic freedom."

Communist Party. Gallacher House, 69 Albert Road, Glasgow GH2 8DP, Scotland.

Dionnasg Gaidhlig Na h-Alba. 34 Berkeley Street, Glasgow 3, Scotland.

> "Membership of the Gaelic League of Scotland is open to all prepared to strive for a Gaelic-speaking Scotland and a revival of Gaelic culture.

Edinburgh Public Library. The Scottish Room, George IV Bridge, Edinburgh EH1 1EW, Scotland.

John MacLean Society. Atholl Cottage, Bathgate Road, Westfield, West Lothian, EH48 3DF, Scotland.

> Founded "to commemorate and publicize the life and work of the Scottish Socialist, John MacLean (1879-1923), to publish his writings, letters, and speeches and to relate his life and work to the circumstances of today."

Labour Party. Scottish Council. Keir Hardie House, 1 Lyndoch Place, Glasgow G3 6AB, Scotland.

Mitchell Library. North Street, Glasgow G3 7DN, Scotland.

The National Library of Scotland. George IV Bridge, Edinburgh, EH1 1EW, Scotland.

Saltire Society. Saltire House, 13 Atholl Crescent, Edinburgh EH3 8HA, Scotland.

> The Saltire Society was formed in 1936 "with the object of encouraging Scottish Art, Literature, and Music."

School of Scottish Studies. 27 George Square, Edinburgh EH8 9LD, Scotland.

> Established in 1951 "to collect, study and preserve material relating to culture and society, past and present, throughout Scotland and in Scottish communities overseas; to make the results of this work generally available...Scotland's archive of oral tradition."

Scotland-UN. Dr. S. Kerr, 19 Upper Crofts, Alloway, Ayr, Scotland.

> "To press for recognition of Scotland's right to self-determination."

Scottish Conservative Party. 11 Atholl Place, Edinburgh, EH3 8HA. Scotland.

Scottish Information Office. New St. Andrew's House, Edinburgh EH1 3TD. Scotland.

Scottish International Institute. 58 Queen St. Edinburgh EH2 3NS, Scotland.

> Established 1976 with the goal "to furthering research, publication, and other activities relating to the culture and politics of self-government."

Scottish Labour History Society.21 Liberton Brae, Edinburgh EH16 6AQ, Scotland.

Scottish Liberal Party.4 Clifton Terrace, Edinburgh, EH12 5DR Scotland.

Scottish National Dictionary Association.27 George Square, Edinburgh EH8 9LD, Scotland.

   Aim: "to further the study of Scottish language and
   literature."

Scottish National Party. 6 North Charlotte St. Edinburgh EH2 4JH, Scotland.

Scottish Poetry Library Association. Tweeddale Court, 14 High Street, Edinburgh EH1 ITE, Scotland.

   "a place for poetry in Scotland, central, accessible to
   everyone; a comprehensive collection of Scots, Gaelic,
   and English verse, available both for reference and for
   borrowing..."

Scots Language Society. Alex Scott, 14 Kirklee Terrace, Glasgow G12 OTH, Scotland.

   The Society "exists to promote Scots in literature,
   drama, the media, education and in everyday usage."

Scots Secretariat. Jess Cottage, Carlops, Penicuik, Midlothian EH26 9NF, Scotland.

SCRAM Scottish Campaign to Resist the Atomic Menace. 11 Forth St. Edinburgh EH1 3LE, Scotland.

ADDRESSES OF SELECTED PERIODICALS

Books in Scotland. (Quarterly) Ramsay Head Press, 36 N. Castle St. Edinburgh EH2 3 BN, Scotland.

CARN (Quarterly) 9 Br. Cnoc Sion, Dublin 9, Ireland.

Cencrastus. (Quarterly) 5 Buccleuch Place, Edinburgh EH8 9LW, Scotland.

Chapman.(Quarterly) 35 East Claremont Street, Edinburgh EH7 4HT, Scotland.

Gairm (Gaelic Quarterly) 29 Waterloo St. Glasgow G2, Scotland.

Glasgow Herald. (Daily newspaper) 195 Albion Street, Glasgow
G1 IQP, Scotland.

New Edinburgh Review.(Quarterly) 1 Buccleuch Place, Edinburgh
EH8 9LW, Scotland.

New Shetlander.4 B Market Street, Lerwick ZE1 OJN, Shetland,
Scotland.

Radical Scotland. (six issues per annum) 1 Buccleuch Place,
Edinburgh EH8 9LW, Scotland.

Scots Independent (Monthly) 51 Cowane St. Stirling, Scotland.

Scotsman. (Daily newspaper) 20 N. Bridge St. Edinburgh
EH1 1QG, Scotland.

Scottish Review.(Quarterly) 24 George St. Glasgow G2 IEF,
Scotland.

APPENDIX III.

CHRONOLOGY

1707 Jan. 16. Treaty of Union with England
      March 25. Scottish Parliament meets for the last time.
      May 1. Union of the Parliaments of Scotland and England.

1868 James Connolly born in Edinburgh.

1879 John MacLean born in Glasgow.

1885 Highland Land League founded.

1886 Scottish Home Rule Association founded, Keir Hardie
      and Cunninghame-Graham are key members.

1888 Scottish Labour Party formed. First true Labour Party
      in Great Britain.

1892 August 11. Christopher Murray Grieve ("Hugh MacDiarmid")
      born in Langholm, Scotland.

1893 Independent Labour Party founded.

1897 Scottish Trade Union Congress founded.

1900 Young Scots Society founded to promote Home Rule and to
      fight for freedom of speech.
      British Labour Party founded.

1901 Scotland's population stands at $4\frac{1}{2}$ million.

1911 Scottish National League, "Comunn nan Albannach"
      founded by Ruaridh Erskine.

1913 Important Home Rule Bill passes second reading in
      Parliament.

1914 Aug. 4. Britain enters World War I.

1916 Scottish Trade Union Congress passes resolution
supporting Home Rule for Scotland.
Irish Rebellion. James Connolly is executed on May 12 in
Dublin.

1918 Home Rule is a major feature of the Labour Party's
manifesto.

1919 Scottish Conservative Members of Parliament issue two
reports supporting some measure of devolution for
Scotland.

1923 Nov. 30. John MacLean dies in Glasgow.

1924 Jan. 22. Britain's first Labour Government under
Ramsay MacDonald.

1925 The National Library of Scotland Act, creating a
National Library for Scotland.

1926 Hugh MacDiarmid's Drunk Man Looks at the Thistle appears.
General Strike, May 3-May 13.
Lewis Spence founds the Scottish National Movement.

1927 A separate Scottish PEN chapter is founded by C.M.
Grieve, giving Scotland international recognition.

1928 The National Party of Scotland is formed by a merger of
the Glasgow University Scottish Nationalist Association,
The Scottish Home Rule Association, the Scots National
League, and the Scottish National Movement.

1931 Running as a Scottish Nationalist, Compton Mackenzie
is voted Rector of Glasgow University.

1932 28% of Scotland's work force is unemployed.
Scottish Daily Express poll finds 113,000 Scots in
favor of Home Rule and only 5,000 against.
On July 31, the mainly Scottish Independent Labour Party
breaks away from the mainstream British Labour Party.

1933 Hugh MacDiarmid is expelled from the National Party for
his communistic beliefs.

1934 The Scottish National Party is formed by merger between
the National Party of Scotland and the Scottish Party.
The Scots Anti-Conscription League is formed.

1936 The Saltire Society is founded.
Edwin Muir's controversial Scott and Scotland appears,
challenging the notion of a true Scottish Renaissance.

1937 The Annual Conference of the Scottish National Party endorses anti-conscription.

1938 16% of the Scottish work force is unemployed.

1939 Sept. 3. Britain enters World War II.
Scottish Office transferred from London to Edinburgh.

1941 Tom Johnston, Scottish Nationalist and socialist, made Secretary of State for Scotland.

1942 Hugh MacDiarmid re-joins the Scottish National Party. The Scottish National Party splits into factions over the nature of war support to be given to England. Moderates under John MacCormick form the Scottish Convention. Many Scottish Nationalists face tribunals for their anti-war activities.

1945 First Scottish Nationalist election victory. Robert McIntyre captures the seat for Motherwell.

1949 The Kirriemuir Plebiscite- a poll in which 92% of all Scots polled were in favor of some form of self-government.
The Scottish Covenant petition begins circulation, asking Scots to indicate their support for Home Rule for Scotland. Although disputed, nearly $2\frac{1}{2}$ million signatures were gathered within two years, indicating broad popular support for Home Rule in Scotland.

1950 The Stone of Scone, the ancient coronation stone of Scottish kings, was taken from Westminster by Scottish Nationalists. Although the Stone of Scone was returned later in 1951, the act gained much support for Scottish Nationalism in Scotland and abroad.

1952 A "Scottish Declaration" petition circulated by the Covenant Association, to gather support for Home Rule under federalism. "Declaration" not successful.

1967 Next nationalist victory at the polls, with Winifred Ewing winning the seat for Hamilton in the November by-election.

1971 The 1971 census reveals 88,415 Gaelic speakers in Scotland.

1972 Lallans Society founded, with MacDiarmid as president, to further the Scots Language.

1974 The Scottish National Party gains 30.4% of the vote and gains 11 Parliamentary seats in the October General Election.

1975 Sept. James Sillars, MP for South Ayrshire, and John Robertson, MP for Paisley, found the Scottish Labour Party.

1978 September. Hugh MacDiarmid dies.

1979 Referendum held on March 1 asking Scots to vote for or reject a Scottish Assembly. Although a majority voted for an Assembly, fewer than the required 40% voted for the referendum.
Socialist members of the Scottish National Party break away to form the "79 Group."
The Campaign for a Scottish Assembly is formed.

1982 The SNP expels left-wing members of the 79 Group.
The Scottish Trade Union Congress calls for devolution in order to help generate industrial revival in Scotland.

1983 General Election . 2 Scottish Nationalist Members of Parliament are returned. Conservatives win by an impressive majority in England but remain the minority party in Scotland.

INDEX

The numbers below refer to page numbers.

About the Compiler

GORDON BRYAN is Deputy Librarian at the Chester College of Further Education in Chester, England. His studies have appeared in *The Scots Magazine, Irish Studies in Britain,* and other periodicals.